'Never, frankly, can there have been a more blasphemous book. This memoir makes *The God Delusion* look like a parish newsletter'   *Independent on Sunday*

'Unforgettable . . . [Auslander is] America's hottest, funniest, most controversial young Jewish memoirist . . . I challenge even the most disapproving of his parents' friends to read this blackly hilarious, groundbreaking memoir without wiping tears of both kinds from their eyes'   *The Times*

'Hilarious and devastating . . . Few books really are laugh-out-loud funny. This one is. The comic timing is perfect and, as with all the best Jewish jokes, the pain behind the humour is apparent . . . Fascinating'
                                        Naomi Alderman, *Sunday Times*

'It's one of the funniest books I've ever read, killingly so given that, with only a slight adjustment of tone, it could well be read as a practical manual on how to turn out fanatical fundamentalists in the respectable suburbs of New Jersey'   *Observer*

'Outrageously funny . . . Dazzling . . . Raw brilliance infused with classic Jewish irony . . . This is indeed a lament, but a lament with attitude'   *Sunday Telegraph*, Seven

'Auslander may feel he has failed as a Jew, but as a memoirist he is peerless: this is one of the funniest, darkest, rudest accounts of man and God ever written'
                            Sunday Telegraph Summer Reading Special

Foreskin's Lament

Shalom Auslander was raised as an Orthodox Jew in Spring Valley, New York. His writing has been published in the *New Yorker* and *Esquire*, among other magazines. His first book, *Beware of God*, is also published by Picador. He lives in upstate New York with his wife and son.

ALSO BY SHALOM AUSLANDER

Beware of God: Stories

Foreskin's Lament

A Memoir

SHALOM AUSLANDER

PICADOR

First published 2007 as a Riverhead Book by the Penguin Group (USA)

First published in Great Britain 2008 by Picador

First published in paperback 2009 by Picador
an imprint of Pan Macmillan Ltd
Pan Macmillan, 20 New Wharf Road, London N1 9RR
Basingstoke and Oxford
Associated companies throughout the world
www.panmacmillan.com

ISBN 978-0-330- 45354-7

Grateful acknowledgment is made to the *New Yorker,* where portions
of this book originally appeared, in slightly different form.

Photographs: Vincent Oliver/Getty Images; Nick Daly/Getty Images;
Holly Harris/Getty Images; Daly & Newton/Getty Images;
Mario Tama/Getty Images; Bert Loewenherz/Getty Images.

Throughout this book, the names of some places as well as
individuals and their personal details have been changed.

While the author has made every effort to provide accurate telephone numbers
and Internet addresses at the time of publication, neither the publisher nor the
author assumes any responsibility for errors, or for changes that occur after
publication. Further, the publisher does not have any control over and does not
assume any responsibility for author or third-party websites or their content.

1 3 5 7 9 8 6 4 2

A CIP catalogue record for this book is available from
the British Library.

Printed and bound in the UK by
CPI Mackays, Chatham ME5 8TD

Visit **www.picador.com** to read more about all our books
and to buy them. You will also find features, author interviews and
news of any author events, and you can sign up for e-newsletters
so that you're always first to hear about our new releases.

4. And the Lord said unto Moses,
"This is the land I promised you,
but you shall not enter. Psych."
5. And Moses died.

DEUTERONOMY

1.

When I was a child, my parents and teachers told me about a man who was very strong. They told me he could destroy the whole world. They told me he could lift mountains. They told me he could part the sea. It was important to keep the man happy. When we obeyed what the man had commanded, the man liked us. He liked us so much that he killed anyone who didn't like us. But when we didn't obey what he had commanded, he didn't like us. He hated us. Some days he hated us so much, he killed us; other days, he let other people kill us. We call these days "holidays." On Purim, we remembered how the Persians tried to kill us. On Passover, we remembered how the Egyptians tried to kill us. On Chanukah, we remembered how the Greeks tried to kill us.

—Blessed is He, we prayed.

As bad as these punishments could be, they were nothing compared to the punishments meted out to us by the man himself. Then there would be famines. Then there would be floods. Then there would be furious vengeance. Hitler might have killed the Jews, but this man drowned the world. This was the song we sang about him in kindergarten:

> *God is here,*
> *God is there,*
> *God is truly*
> *everywhere!*

Then snacks, and a fitful nap.

I was raised like a veal in the Orthodox Jewish town of Monsey, New York, where it was forbidden to eat veal together with dairy. Having eaten veal, one was forbidden to eat dairy for six hours; having eaten dairy, one was forbidden to eat veal for three hours. One was forbidden to eat pig forever, or at least until the Messiah arrived; it was then, Rabbi Napier had taught us in the fourth grade, that the wicked would be punished, the dead would be resurrected, and pigs would become kosher.

—Yay! I said, high-fiving my best friend, Dov.

—You should be so excited, said Rabbi Napier, peering with disgust over the top of his thick horn-rimmed glasses, —on the Day of God's Judgment.

The people of Monsey were terrified of God, and they taught me to be terrified of Him, too—they taught me about a woman named Sarah who would giggle, so He made her barren; about a man named Job who was sad and asked, —Why?, so God came down to the Earth, grabbed Job by the collar, and howled, —Who the fuck do you think you are?; about a man named Moses, who escaped from Egypt, and who roamed through the desert for forty years in search of a Promised Land, and whom God killed just before he reached it—face-plant on the one-yard line—because Moses had sinned, once, forty years earlier. His crime? Hitting a rock. And so, in early autumn, when the leaves choked, turned colors, and fell to their deaths, the people of Monsey gathered together in synagogues across the town and wondered, aloud and in unison, how God was going to kill them: —*Who will live and who will die,* they prayed, —*who at his predestined time and who before his time, who by water and who by fire, who by sword, who by beast, who by famine, who by thirst, who by storm, who by plague, who by strangulation, and who by stoning.*

Then lunch, and a fitful nap.

It is Monday morning, six weeks after my wife and I learned that she is pregnant with our first child, and I am stopped at a traffic light. The kid doesn't have a chance. It's a trick. I know this God; I know how He works. The baby will be miscarried, or die during childbirth, or my wife will die during childbirth, or they'll both die during childbirth, or neither of them will die and I'll think I'm in the clear, and then on the drive home from the hospital, we'll collide head-on with a drunk driver and they'll both die later, my wife and child, in the emergency room just down the hall from the room where only minutes ago we stood so happy and alive and full of promise.

That would be so God.

The teachers from my youth are gone, the parents old and mostly estranged. The man they told me about, though—he's still around. I can't shake him. I read Spinoza. I read Nietzsche. I read *National Lampoon*. Nothing helps. I live with Him every day, and behold, He is still angry, still vengeful, still—eternally—pissed off.

—Man plans, my parents said, —and God laughs.

—When you least expect it, my teachers warned, —expect it.

And I do. All day long, a never-ending horror film festival plays in my mind, my own private Grand Guignol. There isn't an hour of the day that goes by without some gruesome, horrific imaginings of death, anguish, and torment. Walking down the street, shopping for groceries, filling the truck with gas; friends die, beloveds are murdered, pets are run over by delivery trucks and killed.

Up ahead, past the intersection where the road bends sharply to the right, cars slow, brake lights flashing as they disappear around the bend. An accident, I imagine, and I imagine driving by—*Shithead,* I will criticize the driver, *ought to know better than to speed around here . . .* —when I recognize the car. It is a black Nissan. —*That looks like Orli's . . .* And then I see my wife behind the wheel, crushed, bloody, head back, tongue out. She is dead. I can bring myself to tears this way; if I'm in a particularly self-loathing mood, I may, like a Reuters photographer, place a child's toy in her blood-soaked lap, or a colorfully gift-wrapped box on the dash above the very spot where her head had bashed it in.

Exterior—Daytime—Later. I am sitting on the guardrail, inconsolable.

—You're still young, says a police officer. —Whole life ahead of you.

—She was pregnant, I whisper.

Close-up on the face of the hardened police officer. He has seen it all. But this . . .

A tear rolls down his face.

Fin.

Our unborn baby is the newest star of my horror shows. Just six weeks now since conception and already it's been deformed, deranged, diseased, miscarried, misdiagnosed, mistaken for a tumor and irradiated, sat on, bumped into, impaled during some ill-advised late-term sex, and over-cooked when Orli fell asleep in a steaming bath.

—Are you sure about this? I had asked her as she sank with a sigh into the tub. —Seems a little hot.

—Get out, she had said.

I dragged my finger through the steam that had formed on the shower glass.

—You don't have to make it easy for Him, I said.

—Get OUT.

When I was young, they told me that when I died and went to Heaven, the angels would take me into a vast museum full of paintings I had never before seen, paintings that would have been created by all the artistic sperms I had wasted in my life. Then the angels would take me into a huge library full of books I had never read, books that would have been written by all the prolific sperms I had wasted in my life. Then the angels would take me to a huge house of worship, filled with hundreds of thousand of Jews, praying and studying, Jews that would have been born if I hadn't killed them, wasted them, mopped them up with a dirty sock during the hideous failure of my despicable life (there are roughly 50 million sperms in every ejaculate; that's about nine Holocausts in every wank. I was just hitting puberty when they told me this, or puberty was just hitting me, and I was committing genocide, on average, three or four times a day). They told me that when I died and went to Heaven, I would be boiled alive in giant vats filled with all the semen I had wasted during my life. They told me that when I died and went to Heaven, all the souls of every sperm I wasted during my life would chase me for eternity through the firmament. You don't have to be ordained to play this game—go on, try it!—all you need is terror, bloodlust, and a sense of gruesome, violent irony. Here's mine: I worry that God puts all the healthy, perfect, talented sperm in the early ejaculates of a man's life—the man's someday reward for the control he has had over his revolting animus—and that, as the years pass and he ejaculates again and again (and again and again and again), sperm quality plummets: by the time he is me, all that's left are the rejects—the cross-eyed, the bucktoothed, the overbitten, the underbitten, the flippered of foot, the webbed of finger, the idiots, the lazy, the criminals, the morons, the yutzes, the putzes, the schmucks. That would be so God.

I was at my office, working on some nonfiction stories, when Orli came by to tell me the news.

—I'm pregnant! she shouted.

We kissed, we wept, we held each other tightly; she, I suppose, imagining pink bows, lullabies, and baby booties, as I imagined kneeling beside a hospital delivery bed, sobbing, mother and child dead.

—This almost never happens, the nurse would say, pulling the bloody gloves from her hand and tossing them into the bin. She pats me on the shoulder, and I look up. Our eyes meet. She wrinkles her nose.

—We're gonna need the room soon, hon, she says.

The stories I had been working on were about my life under the thumb of an abusive, belligerent god, a god who awoke millennia ago on the wrong side of the firmament and still hasn't cheered up. Working title: *God Walks Beside Me with a .45 in My Ribs.*

I'd already written more than 350 pages.

—Let's go out tonight, said Orli, we'll celebrate.

We kissed, we hugged, we wept some more, and as soon as Orli had gone, I sat down at my computer, sighed, and dragged all 350 pages of my stories into the computer's trash.

Are you sure, the computer asked me, *you want to remove the items in the Trash permanently? You cannot undo this action.*

I was sure.

There was no need to provoke Him. I've been on God's chessboard long enough to know that every move forward, every bit of good news—Success! Marriage! Child!—is just another Godly gambit, a feign, a fake, a setup; it seems as if I'm making my way across the board, but soon enough God calls check, and the company that hired me goes under, the wife dies, the baby chokes to death. God's pick-and-roll. The Rope-a-Lordy-Dope. God was here, God was there, God was everywhere.

—I'm telling you, Mouse A says, —that fucking cheese is wired.

—Would you stop? whines Mouse B. —You're such a pessi-*zzzzap*.

I wonder if by having a baby, I'm only falling into their trap—God's, my family's, Abraham's, Isaac's, Joseph's—of continuing the cycle, of bringing another child to the altar. *Be fruitful and multiply,* saith the Lord, *and I'll take it from there.*

The traffic light is still red, and my mind wanders. It wanders into the graveyard, it strolls into the morgue, it meanders into Bergen-Belsen:

Something is wrong with the baby.

Something is right now, at this very moment, as I'm sitting here at this traffic light, twirling a stray eyebrow hair and picking at the rubber steering-wheel cover, right now something within my unborn child is failing to develop properly—the something is not getting enough whatever, the whatever is not getting enough something, some cell is failing to split, some other cell is splitting too much.

A few days ago, I resumed work on my God stories. I'm pushing my luck, I know, but if this child somehow lives, I want him or her to know where I come from, why I haven't taught him or her what they taught me, why I have, as my mother put it in one of her last ever e-mails to me, forsaken my people. I know that God knows what I've written so far, and I know that He knows that He's coming off like an asshole—He also knows it's only going to get worse before I am done, and He's doing everything He can to stop me from finishing. Killing me? Too obvious. Murdering the very child for whom I'm writing the book? That would be so God. I imagine there is a tall black building in downtown heaven—lots of steel and concrete, very corporate, with a piazza for smokers out front and a cafeteria on the third floor—a building that is the universal headquarters for God's Department of Ironic Punishmentation, the place where they work out just this kind of hilarious twist. This is where writers go when they die—the novelists, the poets, the sitcom writers, the stand-up comedians—to a steel desk and a hard chair in a tiny cubicle in the DIP, where every human story needs its own original ending, but where every ending is satisfyingly the same: horrible.

The driver behind me leans on her horn. The light has turned green. I drive up around the bend where the cars have been slowing to pass a jogger trudging along by the side of the road. No accident, no dead wife. Not yet, anyway, not today. I drive by, relieved for a moment, but only for a moment, before imagining that the jogger was my friend Roy, and that as soon as I turn off this road and head up the next, Roy, somewhere behind me, will be hit by a truck and killed. A delivery truck. A delivery truck on its way to Roy's house. Delivering—wait—his pornography. *Ha-ha,* they will laugh at the DIP, *that'll learn 'im.* Somebody will get a raise. There will be cake in the cafeteria. If I've met you and liked you at all, I've imagined you dead, decapitated, dismembered.

—You're punishing yourself, says Ike. Ike is my psychiatrist.

—I know, I answer.

—You haven't done anything wrong, he says.

—I know, I answer.

Ike says something further, but I'm not listening. I'm imagining the call from his sobbing wife.

—Ike's dead, she says.

—I know, I answer.

And I know how:

Horribly.

2.

*R*abbi Kahn walked into our third-grade classroom, hung up his long black coat, took off his big black hat, and handed each student a small black booklet titled *The Guide to Blessings.*

We had one week, he told us, to prepare for the annual Yeshiva of Spring Valley Blessing Bee.

My heart leaped.

This was just what my mother needed: my winning the blessing bee would make her forget all the troubles of our home—to have a son who was a *talmid chuchum,* a wise student, that was the ultimate achievement. Her brother was a respected rabbi, and if her husband couldn't be one, maybe her son could be.

The Guide to Blessings was a seventy-page listing of hundreds of different foods, divided into different chapters: Soups, Breads, Fish, Desserts. I flipped through it, slowly realizing the size of the challenge that lay before me, and quickly becoming famished.

Falafel?

Herring?

Eggplant parmigiana?

I had my work cut out for me.

Friday afternoons, the yeshiva closed early so that we could all rush home to help our parents prepare for *Shabbos,* the Sabbath. Rabbi Kahn told us that the Sages tell us that the Torah tells us that the preparation for Sabbath is equal to the importance of Sabbath itself. Most of my preparations involved searching the house for kosher wine and pouring it down the toilet. It was a thankless job I admitted to nobody. My father's frustrated rage at not having his Manischewitz Concord Grape was fearsome, but it was far better than his drunken rage if he did have it. I'd search the pantry, I'd search the garage, I'd search my father's closet. But I was only eight years old, and there was always a bottle of Kedem hiding somewhere I just hadn't thought to check.

That night, my father, drunk on a bottle of blush Chablis that had gotten away, grabbed my older brother by his shirt collar and dragged him away from the Sabbath table. He dragged him all the way down the stairs to our bedroom in the basement and slammed the door shut. Even the silverware jumped.

—Who wants the last matzoh ball? my mother asked. —I made extra.

When my brother returned to the table, his nose was bleeding. My mother brought him a can of frozen orange juice to hold against the back of his neck, which was supposed to somehow stop the flow.

Rabbi Kahn taught us that it is prohibited to defrost frozen orange juice on Sabbath, because changing food from solid to liquid is considered cooking, and cooking is considered working, and even the Lord refrained from working on Sabbath. Of the thirty-nine categories of work that are prohibited on Sabbath, cooking is category 7. That's why you're not allowed to switch on lights—the electricity causes the filament to glow, which is considered burning, which is considered working (category 37).

My father came back to the table and drunkenly sang a few Sabbath songs, fudging the words and banging heavily on the table with his fist. I sat hunched over, absentmindedly drawing circles on the condensation that formed on the silver water pitcher. My father slapped my hand—*Shabbos!* he shouted (writing, category 5). Eventually, he stumbled off to his bedroom and fell asleep, snoring loudly as we sat in the dining room and picked glumly at our food.

The following Monday morning, as we all sat studying from our blessing books, there was a knock on Rabbi Kahn's classroom door, and Rabbi Goldfinger, the yeshiva principal, solemnly entered. We all rose. The two rabbis conferred quietly for a moment before signaling us all to be seated. After a few thoughtful strokes of his long black beard, Rabbi Goldfinger sighed deeply and informed us that the night before, our classmate Avrumi Gruenembaum's father had suffered a heart attack and died.

Some kids have all the luck.

—Blessed is the One True Judge, said Rabbi Kahn, nodding his head.

—Blessed is the One True Judge, we all answered, nodding our heads.

I wondered what Mr. Gruenembaum might have done to deserve death. Had he bowed down to idols? Had he walked four steps without his yarmulke on? Whatever it was, it must have been pretty bad.

As Rabbi Goldfinger turned to leave, he paused and, with a stern shake of his finger, reminded us all that the Sages tell us that the Torah tells us that until the age of thirteen, all of a boy's sins are ascribed to his father.

I turned to look at Avrumi's empty chair. Avrumi was a chubby kid with heavy orthodontia and foul breath, but a sudden respect for him grew within me. I wondered what he might have done to cause his father's death. Whatever it was, it must have been pretty bad.

Scowling fiercely, Rabbi Goldfinger advised each and every one of us to pray to Hashem, the Holy One Blessed Be He, for forgiveness so that He wouldn't decide to kill our fathers, too.

My heart leaped.

—Blessed is Hashem, he said.

—Blessed is Hashem, we answered.

Blessed is Hashem was right—all of a sudden I had two ways I could make everything better. I could win the blessing bee for my mother, and I could sin so much Hashem would have to kill my father.

Courageous Avrumi Gruenembaum. Maybe one *Shabbos* night he had switched on a light. Maybe he drank milk after eating meat. Maybe he touched himself.

That night, just before bed, I ate a drumstick, washed it down with some milk, touched myself, and flicked the bedroom light on and off.

—Break those lights and I'll break your hands! my father shouted.

It was going to be a busy week.

The blessing bee worked the same way as a spelling bee.

There are six basic blessings on food: *hamotzei,* the blessing for bread; *mezonos,* the blessing for wheat; *hagofen,* the blessing for wine or grape juice; *ha-eitz,* the blessing for things that grow from trees; *ho-adamah,* the blessing for things that grow from the earth; and *shehakol,* the blessing for everything else.

Bagel? *Hamotzei.*

Oatmeal? *Mezonos.*

Gefilte fish? *Shehakol,* the blessing for everything else.

But that was the easy part. Things became much more complicated when you started combining foods: some foods are superior to other foods, and in combination with subordinate foods, the superior food gets the blessing. To make matters worse, some blessings are superior to other blessings and you had to know which blessing to recite first. This is where they separated the men from the goys:

Spaghetti and meatballs? *Mezonos,* the wheat blessing, followed by *shehakol,* the everything-else blessing.

Cereal with milk? *Shehakol* for the milk, followed by *mezonos* for the wheat in the cereal.

Twix, the chocolate candy with the cookie crunch? Trick question: Twix isn't kosher. Of course, for a kosher candy bar with fruits, nuts, or other fillings, the blessing depends upon why you ate it. If you ate it specifically because you like the filling, you must recite the appropriate blessing for that filling. However, if you are eating the candy as much for the chocolate as you are for the filling, you must first recite a *shehakol* on the chocolate, followed by the appropriate blessing on the filling.

Theologically speaking, candy wasn't worth it.

I spent the next week sinning and blessing and blessing and sinning, alternately praising God and then defying Him as much as one eight-year-old possibly could.

Monday morning I stuffed myself—I had a bowl of Fruity Pebbles (*mezonos*), a slice of toast (*hamotzei*), a glass of juice (*shehakol*), half an apple (*ha-eitz*), and a couple of old french fries I found at the bottom of the fridge (*ho-adamah*). One meal, five blessings.

Tuesday I touched myself. I also partook of bread without first ceremoniously washing my hands, and that evening, before going to sleep, I sat on the edge of my bed and carefully recited "shit," "fuck," and "ass" a dozen times each.

My father banged angrily on my bedroom door. —Lights out, he barked.

I smiled. For you and me both, pal.

Wednesday I stole five dollars from my mother and didn't recite any blessings at all on the bag full of candy that I bought with it. (A Charleston Chew, which is *traif,* or non-kosher, to begin with, and a Chunky, which would have been a *shehakol* if I weren't trying to kill my father. A Chunky with Raisins would have been *shehakol,* then *ha-eitz.*)

Thursday I didn't wear *tzitzis.* Rabbi Kahn noticed that the strings weren't dangling from my sides, and he grabbed me by the ear and pulled me to the front of the class.

—*Speak to the children of Israel,* he quoted loudly from the Torah as he spanked me hard on my bottom, —*and tell them to make tzitzis on the corners of their garments!*

That afternoon, after both disrespecting my elders by not taking out the garbage as my mother had asked me to, and defiling a prayer book by carrying it into the bathroom, I touched myself—twice—and silently begged God just this once to credit those sins to Rabbi Kahn's account.

The blessing bee was the following morning, and I could hardly sleep. Cornflakes? *Ho-adamah.* Potato knish? *Mezonos.* Root beer. Is it a root? Is it beer? Fuck. Shit. Ass. Bitch.

I tossed and turned, I blessed and cursed, and fell, finally, into an uncomfortable sleep.

After a week at home, Avrumi Gruenembaum conveniently returned to school just in time for the blessing bee. It was all I could do to not lean over and ask him how he did it.

—*Psst. Avrumi. Was it lobster? Did you eat lobster? Side of bacon? Come on, you can tell me.*

Rabbi Kahn told us that the Sages tell us that the Torah tells us that when Abraham died, God comforted Isaac, as it is written in Genesis 25:11, "After Abraham's death, God blessed Isaac." We learn from this that it is a tremendous mitzvah, or good deed, to comfort the bereaved. Rabbi Kahn instructed us all to line up at Avrumi's desk to shake his hand and recite the traditional mourner's consolation: "May God comfort you among the mourners of Zion and Jerusalem." Being just eight years old, I was not yet wholly conversant with God's compensatory system, but it occurred to me that, along with all my sins, my father might also be getting all my good deeds. I wasn't taking any chances.

—May God comfort you among the mourners of Zion and Jerusalem, Dov said to Avrumi.

—May God comfort you among the mourners of Zion and Jerusalem, Motty said to Avrumi.

—How's it going? I said to Avrumi. —Tough break.

Rabbi Kahn pinched the skin of my upper arm between his thumb and forefinger and twisted.

—Ow! I screamed.

—*Shmendrik,* he grumbled. Idiot.

After the last boy had asked God to comfort Avrumi among the mourners of Zion and Jerusalem, Rabbi Kahn raised his hand high above his head and brought it down with a crash upon his desk. Even the prayer books trembled.

The blessing bee began.

We lined up at the back of the classroom, nervously pulling on our *tzitzis* and twirling our *peyis.* The rules were simple: name the correct blessing, and remain standing for the next round. Name the wrong blessing, and you take your seat.

Last year's winner, Yukisiel Zalman Yehuda Schneck, stood beside me. He leaned calmly against the wall, nonchalantly picking his nose. The kid was ice.

—Auslander, Shalom! called out Rabbi Kahn. I stepped forward.

—Apple! he shouted.

—Apple! I called out. —*Ha-eitz!*

—Correct, said Rabbi Kahn.

The blessing bees began easily. Dov Becker got tuna (*shehakol,* the everything-else blessing), Ari Mashinsky got matzoh (*hamotzei,* the blessing for bread), and Yisroel Tuchman got stuck with kugel, which he thought was *ho-adamah*— food from the earth—but really was *mezonos*—the blessing on wheat. Three other kids got taken out by oatmeal, borscht with sour cream claimed two others, and by the end of the first round, almost a third of the students were already back in their seats.

Round two.

—Auslander, Shalom! called out Rabbi Kahn.

I stepped forward.

—Mushroom barley soup! he shouted.

Mushroom barley soup, mushroom barley soup. Damn. I knew I should have studied the chapter on soups more; I'd wasted half the week on entrees.

Was it *ho-adamah* on the mushrooms, which came from the earth, or was it *mezonos* on the barley? Maybe it was *shehakol*, the everything-else blessing, on the liquid? He hadn't said anything about croutons . . . what if there were croutons?

—Mushroom barley soup! I called out. —*Mezonos!*

Rabbi Kahn glared at me and tugged on his beard, his eyes narrowing into angry little slits.

—And . . . uh . . . *shehakol*? I added.

Rabbi Kahn smacked his desk, signaling that I was correct. His expression conveyed a sense of triumph, as if his sneering and unspoken threats alone had been responsible for my success.

Apple strudel took out Dov Becker, Yoel Levine, and Mordechai Pomerantz. My friend Motty Greenbaum got stuck with cheesecake, and I could tell, just by the expression on his face, that he had absolutely no idea. He wisely offered two answers, one for thin crust and one for thick, and somehow managed to stay alive.

It was hard to believe this was only round two.

—Gruenembaum, Avrumi! shouted Rabbi Kahn.

Avrumi stepped forward. I smiled at Motty. Avrumi may have killed his father, but other than that, he wasn't very bright. He was lucky to be in the second round at all.

—Bagel! shouted Rabbi Kahn.

Bagel? I looked at Motty in disbelief. Was he kidding? Bagel?

—Bagel! Avrumi called out. —*Hamotzei!*

This was bullshit.

—Correct! shouted Rabbi Kahn. —Very good!

Ephraim Greenblat, Avrumi Epstein, and Yehosua Frankel all got out on *cholent* with barley and large pieces of meat, while chopped liver on challah with a slice of lettuce and a bit of olive took out four more, including Motty.

And then there were three: it was just Yukisiel Zalman Yehuda Schneck, Avrumi Gruenembaum, and me.

Round three began.

—Auslander, Shalom! called out Rabbi Kahn.

I stepped forward.

—Ice cream, shouted Rabbi Kahn. —In a cone!

Ice cream in a cone, ice cream in a cone. I knew ice cream, but why would he add the cone? Was the blessing different if it was in a cone? What was a cone made from, anyway? Was it cake? Was it a wafer?

—Ice cream in a cone! Rabbi Kahn shouted.

—Uh, hmm . . . is that a sugar cone or is that a regular cone?

—A sugar cone! he shouted. —A sugar cone, of course a sugar cone!

Is the ice cream subordinate to the cone? Is the cone subordinate to the ice cream? Most of the calories came from the ice cream, so perhaps the cone was subordinate to the ice cream? Was it calorie-related? Then again, if it's a sugar cone, maybe you really desire the cone, and then the ice cream is subordinate to the cone? Dear God, were there sprinkles involved?

—ICE CREAM IN A CONE! Rabbi Kahn shouted again.

—Ice cream in a cone! I called out. —No blessing!

Everyone in the classroom turned to face me.

Looking back on the whole episode, Rabbi Kahn had really left me no choice.

—No blessing? said Rabbi Kahn. —Why no blessing?

—Because, I explained, nervously twirling my long white *tzitzis,* —because . . . because the room smells like doody.

There was a long silence. Motty giggled, and others followed. Soon the whole room was filled with laughter. Rabbi Kahn slowly rose to his feet, his thick fists pushing themselves into the desktop.

It may have been a loophole, but technically speaking, I was correct. Rabbi Kahn himself had told us that our Sages tell us that the Torah tells us that there are three situations in which one is absolutely prohibited from reciting a blessing: (1) while facing a male over the age of nine years old whose genitals are showing, (2) while facing a female over the age of three years old whose genitals are showing, and (3) in the presence of feces.

Frankly, given the other two options, I think I chose the least offensive answer.

For a big man, Rabbi Kahn moved pretty quickly.

—It's true, I said as he barreled toward me, —the Torah says that . . .

He grabbed me roughly by my arm, lifting me clear off the ground, and dragged me toward the door, shouting angrily in Yiddish the whole time.

—But it smells like doody! I yelled. —The room smells like doody! Wait! There's a naked girl in the room! There's a naked girl . . . !

The door slammed shut behind me.

I stood in the hallway, rubbed my bruised arm, and began to cry. The blessing bee was lost, I was not a great rabbi, and my father was still not dead.

I tiptoed toward the classroom door and listened closely. Two minutes later, Yukisiel Zalman Yehuda Schneck fell victim to matzoh brei with maple syrup, and the last man standing was Avrumi Gruenembaum.

—Apples! called out Rabbi Kahn.

—Apples, Avrumi answered. —*Ha-eitz!*

—*Mazel tov!* called out Rabbi Kahn. —*Mazel tov!*

Total bullshit.

That night we had the traditional Friday-night gefilte fish (*shehakol*) with a little slice of carrot (*ho-adamah*). My father was drunk again, fudging the words of the Sabbath songs and banging heavily on the table with his fist. My mother went into the kitchen and brought out the soup. When my brother said he didn't want any, my father slapped him and poured the hot chicken soup onto his face and lap.

My mother took my brother into the bathroom and sat with him on the edge of the bathtub, pressing a cold washcloth against his cheeks, and I went back to the dining room to wipe the chicken soup off the floor. Chicken soup is a *shehakol,* even if it is cooked with vegetables, since chicken is the dominant taste in the soup.

Rabbi Kahn told us that the Sages tell us that the Torah tells us that the Holy One Blessed Be He sent the Egyptians ten plagues in order to teach us that He gives people many chances to repent, and only then, if they still continue to sin, does He punish them with death.

I went downstairs to my bedroom, took four steps without my yarmulke on, touched myself, flicked the lights off and on, and fell asleep.

3.

By the time I was eight years old, I had already learned twelve different names for God, not including the One That Must Never Be Said. There was Hashem, El, Adonai, Shadai, He Who Is Full of Mercy, He Who Is Quick to Anger, the Holy Spirit, the Divine Presence, the Rock, the Savior, the Guardian of the Worlds, and He Who Was, He Who Is, and He Who Will Always Be What He Is. One day Rabbi Kahn was teaching us the story of Adam and Eve in the Garden of Eden when he referred to God as "Our Father Who Is in Heaven."

I shuddered.

There's another one? In heaven? *That's* God? Did He stumble around in His underwear? How big was His fist? As big as a car? As big as a house? What was it like to get punched by a house? If someone hit you with a fist as big as a house, you'd probably die, right, I mean, if God ever got drunk . . .

Rabbi Kahn stood behind his desk, a *Chumash,* or Pentateuch, in one hand, his other hand solemnly twisting his beard.

—And God, said Rabbi Kahn, —was very angry.

He shut his eyes, slowly beating the top of his desk with his fist as he shook his head with disappointment. Nobody moved. Nobody spoke. Nobody even breathed.

—ADAM! Rabbi Kahn suddenly shouted. Everyone jumped. Rabbi Kahn rose up on his toes and extended his arm over his head, index finger pointing to the heavens above the drop ceiling above.

—You . . . have . . . SINNED!

Yukisiel slunk down in his chair and picked his nose. Avrumi nervously twirled his *peyis*. I pulled a hair out of the top of my head. Rabbi Kahn slowly opened his eyes.

—Get OUT! he shouted, pointing suddenly to the windows. —GET OUT!

Shmuel started to get up. So did Yoel. Our classroom was on the second floor.

—BOTH OF YOU! he continued. —Get OUT of my Garden of Eden!

Rabbi Kahn glared at me. He glared at everyone. His finger, still pointing to the windows, trembled with furious rage.

I pulled another hair from the top of my head.

All he'd forgotten was the underwear.

I am sitting in a coffee shop in Woodstock, New York, trying, despite the Islamic Jihad's best efforts, to work. I can't help noticing that every time I begin to make some progress on my stories about God, attacks in Israel increase, and I feel guilty and stop. Am I causing these attacks? Is God showing me what it will be like if I piss Him off, if He decides, once again, to let our enemies destroy us? My rabbis taught me that it was wrong to say God caused the Holocaust; that He had simply, in 1938, turned His head. He looked away. *What? Huh? Geno . . . really? Shit, I was in the bathroom.* Not a murderer, just an accessory. Were the day's headlines a silent threat? Am I next? My teachers told me that it is a sin punishable by death from above for a Jew to embarrass the Jewish people, which I am concerned these stories do. But I take a deep breath and remember that Aaron Spelling's doing okay, and if he's not an embarrassment to the Jewish people, I don't know who is.

—What about Aaron? I say to God. —Go bother Aaron.

For the People of the Book, words, being the stuff of books, have weight. Words have consequences. In the beginning was the Word, and the Word was the name of the Lord, and so the second word they came up with, immediately after the Word, was the word Holy, which described the first Word, which you were now prohibited from uttering, even though there were only two words in total, effectively cutting the entire language in half. Soon came the words "shan't" and "mustn't" and "stoning" and "kill," and then a whole lot of other words that you were required to say in case the first Word was uttered, words of penance, apology, and promise that you would never utter that Word in vain again, so help you Word.

Words have weight.

—It sounds like narcissism to me, my friend Craig says of my relationship with God. —Like you're so important.

I imagine us, bound and blindfolded in a dark basement as a masked intruder holds a gun to my head. I'm trembling, panicking, on the edge of tears.

—He's going to kill me, I whisper.

—Jesus Christ, Craig scoffs. —You are really full of yourself.

We were at a bar in Manhattan at the time, and I was concerned God would kill him on his way back to Brooklyn just for having this conversation with me.

—We shouldn't be discussing this here, I said.

He shook his head and laughed.

—You really think God is running around with nothing better to do than fuck with people?

The television above the bar was tuned to CNN. There were bombings in Israel, killings in Gaza, murders in Darfur. Shiites were killing Sunnis, Afghans were killing Pakistanis, Janjaweed were killing everyone. There were heat waves on the West Coast, floods on the East. There were earthquakes, tsunamis, hurricanes, tornadoes, mudslides, diseases old and diseases new—there were syndromes and himdromes and plindromes and shmindromes!

—Yes, I answered him. —I do.

Lately, the person I thought He was fucking with most was me. I was nervous about the forthcoming birth, unsure of how I would raise this child, and terrified that the intro-

duction of this baby into our lives would somehow reintroduce with him or her the families from which we had
worked so long to distance ourselves, a distance I was just
beginning to gain, a distance that had saved my marriage
and my life; I was less volatile, less furious. I was writing. I
was a better husband and about to become a father, and
I was worried that this was God's punch line—the walls of
our world stronger now, the roof solid and secure above our
heads, we decide to open the door to a child, and that in that
opening, the rats and pests of my past scurry inside and bury
themselves in the walls and the beams, and soon the house
collapses.

—A baby, I had said to Ike the week after learning of the
pregnancy.

—So?

—So they're going to want to see him.

—Your responsibility is to your son, he said.

—So, what? I just say no?

—You just say no.

—I'm not sure I can be that big an asshole.

—I believe you can.

—You're a good friend.

A few days later, I ran into an old acquaintance from
Monsey. I told him we were expecting a baby; he'd recently
had a child of his own, and I shared with him my concerns
about my family. He e-mailed me the following day, saying
that I had to accept them. That I had to realize that this child
wasn't just my son, but also their grandchild. That there were

going to be holidays and birthdays, and that I had to accept that I couldn't just cut them out of my life.

—No, I replied.

And cut him out of my life.

The coffee shop this morning is blissfully quiet. It is early morning; the only ones awake at this hour are construction workers, landscapers, and writers. Perhaps it's the silence, perhaps it's the organic Zanzibar double espresso, but I think I've finally figured out the theme connecting all these disparate stories I've been working on: they're basically just stories about one man's desire to . . .

Suddenly there are four of them—breasts—making their way toward me. I have looked up for only a moment, and there they are: two women crossing Tinker Street, heading toward the coffee shop. They are just my type, in that they are almost naked and wearing high heels; white tube tops each, one of them in a short, loose green skirt, the other in a long white one, see-through in the sun rising slowly behind her, the Peeping Tom's sly celestial accomplice. I didn't know who had invented high-heel shoes, but I wondered, as they walked toward me, if he was dead, and what punishment God might be causing him to suffer. Forced to walk in heels for eternity? Tied to a post and beaten with four-inch stilettos by all the furious souls his evil design had caused to be wasted? Or maybe—a DIP special—he's in a world where every woman wears flats? Maybe he's been sent back as a heel of a shoe? Maybe he's one of the heels of these two? One of the women is thin and blond, the other is thick and black.

This is my God—this is El, this is Shadai, this is the Guardian of the World—this is Him, not taking any chances, covering the bases of my myriad perversions. They float across the street, wiggling, jiggling, swinging, swaying, a thousand irresistible movements in every single irresistible step. They would be chased out of Jerusalem, these two; they would be shot in Afghanistan; they would be hanged in Iran. The price of freedom is eternal titillation. They don't belong here in Woodstock, either—this is a small town, I have lived here for more than ten years and I have never seen either of them before; it is as if they materialized, *Star Trek* style, in the middle of the street, as if Kirk had been having a party in the *Enterprise* and a couple of the strippers, looking for the bathroom, stumbled through the transporter room instead.

They are in the coffee shop now. The blonde looks at me and bites her lower lip. The black girl smiles as she passes by.

I look back to my computer. Where was I? Didn't I . . . ? What was . . . ? I thought I'd had it. Something about God? No, that doesn't sound right. Who wants to read about God? Is the blond one smiling at me? Christ Almighty, that black girl is hot. Where . . . where was I?

This is the kind of God I'm dealing with.

4.

One Saturday night, not long after the blessing bee, Rabbi Blonsky phoned my father and asked if he would build a new holy ark for the synagogue.

—He who contributes to the building of a synagogue, Rabbi Blonsky said earnestly, —is considered to have saved the entire Jewish people.

I awoke early the following morning to the familiar tortured wail of my father's radial saw. The garage was next door to my bedroom.

—Cocksucker, I heard my father say.

He was talking to the ark.

Rabbi Blonsky was the rabbi of our local synagogue, a congregation of about fifty families, located in a converted cottage house on Carlton Road. Rabbi Blonsky was forty years old, and he worried a lot about the Jewish people. I was nine years old, and it was the Jewish people in my house I was worried about. A holy ark wasn't going to help any of us.

. . .

I'd been worried for some time now. Two years ago, when I was seven, I worried so much I did Nixon. My father had attacked my brother with the dining room table, trapping him in the corner and shoving the table into my brother's stomach until he couldn't breathe.

—Please, said my mother.

Rabbi Kragoff taught us that when God told Noah that a great storm was coming, and commanded Noah to build the Ark, Noah refused. —Why should I have to save everyone? Noah asked. And so God took Noah, and He showed him how wicked the people in his generation had become, and how they had forgotten God, and how hatred had filled their hearts, and Noah realized that if he didn't save them, nobody would.

Which is why I started doing Nixon.

My family, too, suffered storms, and hatred filled their hearts, and after watching my father trying to kill my brother with the *Shabbos* table, I took upon myself the role of family barometer, the Noah of 7 Arrowhead Lane, forever testing the atmosphere for developing systems of tension and distress. Our home was a suburban, split-level hurricane alley, and when the clouds over our dining room grew heavy with bile and the bickering winds blew again across the table—*Keep it up,* my father would growl at my older brother, fists clenched beside his dinner plate, —*see what it gets you*—I would jump down from my chair and make my way to the foot of the table. Showtime.

—*Gib a keek,* my mother would say to my father. Take a look.

There I would turn, face my family, throw my arms out to the side and quickly draw them back against my ribs in a modified *The Thinker* position, right hand tucked beneath my left elbow, my left hand crooked underneath my chin, and I would walk to the head of the table, head down, shoulders hunched, shaking my head and saying —"I am not a thief, I am not a thief."

—What on earth? my mother would exclaim with desperate laughter.

—He's doing Richard Nixon, my brother would say.

—How does he know from Richard Nixon?

I didn't know from Richard Nixon; I'd seen a man doing this on television a few days earlier. His name was Dan Aykroyd. I didn't know who he was, either, but I knew that everyone had laughed. I thought I was doing Dan Aykroyd.

My father would try his best to remain angry, but a few more Nixons up and down the table, and he would smile, and the storm would pass, and the sky would begin to clear. Soon everyone at the table was laughing, and nobody could remember why they had almost killed each other.

—*Meshuginah* kid, my father would mutter.

—Who wants more chicken? my mother would ask.

—I am not a thief, I would say, —I am not a thief. Everyone loves Nixon.

· · · · ·

Something happened.

I could remember a time—it seemed like a long time ago—when my father and I would play-wrestle before bed. During the winter, while the snow swirled across the street and the wind tore through the trees, he would bundle up and trudge outside to pour water down the hill so that our sled run would be frozen for us in the morning. When the school closings were announced, we cheered and dashed outside to play in the snow, and our sleds would already be waiting for us beside the front door. When spring came, and the birds returned and the flowers bloomed, my father taught me how to swim, and sometimes he let me drive his mower, and on a really good day, the best days of all, we'd go into his garage, close the door behind us, and together we'd build.

My father could build anything. Tables, bookcases, stairs, rooms—rooms!—a whole room, with just a hammer and a saw and the few things he had brought back from his weekly trips to Rickel's Home Improvement Center. In the family room, he put lights inside the ceiling. Not on the ceiling—*inside* the ceiling. How do you put lights *inside* a ceiling? He built a deck, and the summer after that he built walls around that deck, so that the deck became a room, and the summer after that he built another deck on the outside of the room he had built from the deck he had built before. And the things that he built were perfect, and they were beautiful—the edges were sharp and the joints were tight, and never was there a gap or a split or mistake. My rabbis told me I had a *yiddishe kupp,* a Jew head, which meant I was smart (a *goyishe kupp,* or Gentile head, meant you were stupid), but Jew head or not, I could never figure out how my father knew just where to cut, which board to use or how they all fit together so perfectly in the end, as if they had wanted to, as if the boards and glue and nails had just been waiting for him to put them in their proper order. We were Levites, descended from the tribe of Levi: in ancient times, we were the artisans, the craftsmen, the builders. The Levites carried the Tabernacle wherever the Israelites traveled; they built the Tabernacle when they arrived, and they dismantled it when they left. Some Sages said that the Levites built the Tabernacle not with their hands, but with their breath, with their speech, that a Levite need only recite a secret set of sacred words, and the walls and the curtains and doors assembled themselves, but I decided as I watched him build—with his strong hands, his sharp eyes, his tongue peeking out of the corner of his mouth as he lined up a cut on the saw— that it could only be the lazy Levites, the unskilled Levites, the hacks, who would ever lower themselves to use some silly magic words. We built a table for my mother, a bookcase for the dining room. One summer we built a deck together—the deck outside the room that used to be a deck—just the two of us. In the evenings, palms blistered, fingertips filled with satisfying splinters, we barbecued some chicken, salted some corn, and talked about what our next project would be. At the end of the summer, when we had finished the final rails and the stain had dried on the long, perfect stairs, I made him a poster: 100 Things You Can Do Besides Smoking. I worried he was going to die. He was overweight and his hair was gray, and I wanted to stop time and make him live forever.

Now, just a few years later, I worried he might do just that. Something happened.

—What happened? I asked my mother.

—You should never know the pain of losing a child, my mother said.

She was talking about Jeffie. Jeffie was their son. He was two years old when he died of a disease whose name, like Hitler's, was rarely spoken. This was well before I was born, before even my older sister was born.

There was a picture of Jeffie on the wall in the hallway, sitting on a white park bench with my brother. Behind them were fake white trees and some yellow flowers. Jeffie was laughing. He had curly hair like mine.

—Cocksucker, I would say to Jeffie when my family fought. —Look what you did.

An old man died.

—Sad, everyone said, without much sadness.

The man had been very wealthy, and he left the synagogue a large sum of money. Rabbi Blonsky bought himself a new leather chair, the kitchenette got a new refrigerator/freezer,

and the congregation got a brand-new Torah. Torahs are written by hand, take months to finish, and cost thousands of dollars to buy. The congregation already had two Torahs, but
they were old: one of them smelled funny, but nobody ever
mentioned it because it had survived the Holocaust. (One
Saturday morning, unable to wiggle my way out of it, I was
called up to the *bimah,* or altar, to help close the Torah after it
had been lifted by the cantor for everyone in the synagogue to
see. This involved rolling the parchment back around the
spools, tying it with an elastic buckle, slipping the velvet cover
over it, and kissing it before hurrying back to my seat.

—I'm so proud of you, my mother said after services ended.

—That Torah smells funny.

—That Torah survived the Holocaust.

—So?

—So have some respect.

—It stinks.

—I'd like to see how you'd smell after a Holocaust.)

Torahs were kept at the front of the synagogue in the holy
ark, the holiest place in the synagogue, the place where the
Holy Spirit of God comes to rest during prayers. Unfortunately, as Rabbi Blonsky had explained to my father that night
on the phone, the synagogue's current holy ark had room for
only two Torahs, so that, along with their brand-new Torah,
the synagogue would need a brand-new holy ark.

—Hidden costs, Rabbi Blonsky had joked.

And they would need it, he added—built, stained, and
installed—in just three weeks.

. . . .

I waited for the radial saw to resume wailing, and when it did, I climbed out of bed, trying not to make a sound. Along with their craftsmanship, Levites were also known for their anger. Levi himself was prone to fits of violence and rage so fearsome that his father, Jacob, refused to make him his heir. He tried to kill his brother Joseph. He slaughtered the entire Hivite nation. After the sin of the golden calf, it was the Levites Moses chose to ride through the camp and kill all the idolaters. *And the Levites did as Moses commanded, and that day about three thousand of the people died.*

—Piece of shit, growled my father as I tiptoed past the garage door.

He was talking to his hammer.

My father still built things, and the things that he built were still perfect and beautiful, but he built them with less and less patience and more and more fury. The wood seemed terrified of him now, tense, like livestock before a slaughter; boards that once gave themselves to him now resisted, the floor of the garage littered with their butchered remains, a massacre of maple and pine.

Something happened.

—What happened? I had asked my mother.

—His sisters, she had said. —They were very mean to him. When he was little.

I trudged upstairs to the kitchen, where the rest of my family were having breakfast, knowing that my mother would ask me to spend the day helping my father. Perhaps if she had ever seen him have a go at a stubborn nail with the sharp end of a claw-tooth hammer she would have reconsidered. The Hivites had gotten off easy. I found her sitting at the kitchen table with my brother and sister and tried my best not to make eye contact, sitting across from her and pretending to read the back of the cereal box just as we all pretended not to hear my father downstairs, swearing his way through another ill-fated acre of lumber.

—What's a cocksucker? my brother asked.

—Watch your language, my mother said.

—*Shit!*

My brother smiled.

—Well, I'll be, said my mother, pretending to read from the local newspaper. —Caldor's is having a sale on linens.

—*Jesus H. Christ!*

—Ten ninety-nine, she continued. —That's a good buy.

I tried to help.

—Seventeen essential vitamins and minerals, I read aloud from the back of the Cheerios box. —That's a lot. I mean, it's not just a lot of essential vitamins and minerals for a breakfast cereal to have, but it's a lot of vitamins and minerals to be considered essential, if you see what I mean, it makes you think about how fragile we . . .

—*Balls!*

My sister didn't say very much at all. My brother could be relentlessly Levite toward her, and if she said or did anything, he would pick on her until she cried. Silence became her Nixon. Instead of talking, she ate, and my brother teased her about it and called her fat.

—Why do I have to sit across from her? he asked. —She's gross.

—*Son of a fucking bitch!*

—Thiamin *and* niacin, I said. —Honestly, it would be a bargain if it had just one . . .

—Why don't you go help your father? my mother asked me.

—Ha-ha, teased my older brother, flicking my ear with his index finger.

—Stop it, said my mother. —He's not so bad.

Terrifying sounds of destruction rose up from the garage—hammers striking nails, pine splintering, heavy oak being thrown to the floor and cursed. A lumber Holocaust. —*Never again,* the maple moaned. —*Never again.*

—Then *you* help him, my brother said to my mother.

—What do I know about building? she answered. —Besides, are you going to do the laundry?

—I'll do the laundry, I offered. —I like doing laundry.

—*Cocksucker!*

—I don't like the way you fold towels, she said. —Why don't you go help your father?

—But Ephraim is coming over, I said.

—He can come over next Sunday, said my mother.

—Yeah, said my brother, flicking my ear again. —Ephraim can come over next Sunday.

Suddenly I felt bad for my father. I wondered what it

would be like if nobody in your family wanted to help you build a holy ark. If they bickered about who had to spend time with you. If they secretly wished that your hand would slip while you were feeding lumber through the saw and you would fall into the blade and get cut into a billion pieces.

Goddamnit, I thought.

—Okay, I said.

—Ha-ha, teased my brother.

—Good boy, said my mother.

Eventually, even Nixon stopped working.

—But I don't want the stupid soup, my brother would say.

—You'll eat what your mother gives you, my father would grumble.

—Please, my mother would say to my brother, —just try a little.

—Give it to fatso, my brother would say, motioning toward my sister.

—You'll eat it, my father would growl, —or you'll wear it.

I'd leap off my dinner chair, throw my arms out to the side, and quickly drew them back in. Showtime.

—I am not a thief, I would say. —I am not—

—Sit your ass down, my father would grumble.

I needed new material.

I saw another man on the show with Dan Aykroyd. His name was Steve, and he had an arrow through his head. —I'm a wild and crazy guy, he said. —A wild and *craaazy* guy.

Everyone laughed.

I didn't get it. Besides, even if I could figure out how he got the arrow through his head, bringing a weapon to our Sabbath table didn't seem like a very good idea. The challah knife had me worried enough.

So I spilled things.

A cup of wine. A glass of soda. The water pitcher. The bottle of borscht.

—You watch your goddamn mouth, my father would say to my brother.

—Look who's talking, my brother would answer.

—Please, my mother begged.

—Whoops! I would cry out, knocking over my glass.

My mother would run for the paper towels. My father would leap for the prayer books. My sister would dive for the kugel platter. Everyone was doing something—even if that something was yelling at me—but nobody was fighting.

It was a messy few months. Plates of gefilte fish. Trays of chicken. Noodle kugel platters, potato kugel platters, onion kugel platters. Bowls of carrot *tzimmis*. For a short while, it worked even better than Nixon.

—The tablecloth's stained, grumbled my father.

—The kugel's ruined, whined my mother.

Nobody's bleeding, I thought.

Rabbi Napier told us that it took Noah 120 years to build his ark, and that all the while he would tell people that a flood was coming, that God was angry, but they wouldn't repent, and they wouldn't change their ways.

—Some people just can't be saved, Noah said.

My mother began keeping all the platters away from me. No cups, no mugs, no goblets. Even my plate was paper.

—Klutz, she would say.

Some people just can't be saved.

I finished my breakfast and walked into the garage just as my father was throwing another piece of lumber onto the scrap pile in the corner.

—Son of a, said my father. He was talking to his bar clamp.

He slid his yarmulke back onto the top of his head and wiped a heavy forearm across his furious brow.

—Hand me the try square, he said without turning around. —Today.

A try square is a triangular ruler with a square corner and a raised edge. It is used for measuring and marking trim lines on wood. I didn't know what a cocksucker was.

—What's a crowbar for? I asked.

This was my new tactic, now that my access to liquids was restricted and spilling no longer worked: random questions about woodworking, precision-timed to achieve maximum emotional distraction. God tended to fly off the handle when people in the Torah asked him questions, but I hoped things would be different with my father on Earth.

—For cracking you over the skull, he said. —Now hand me the try square.

It was no Nixon.

—Wracked, he said, throwing another wooden corpse to the ground. Boards that were wracked were twisted and couldn't be used. He pulled on his shirt, grabbed his cigarettes, and refastened his yarmulke to his hair.

—WE'RE GOING TO RICKEL'S, he shouted up to my mother. —Let's go, he then muttered to me.

I followed him out to the driveway, taking one last hopeful glance back at the house. Upstairs, at her bedroom window, my mother waved to me.

—Go, she silently mouthed. —Go.

My brother stood behind her, pointing at me and laughing. Suddenly I felt bad for my father. I wondered what it would be like if none of your sons wanted to go to Rickel's with you. If your wife had to beg them to help you. If they secretly wished that you would get in your car and go to Rickel's and never come back.

—*Goddamnit,* I thought.

And got in his car.

—Move your ass! my father shouted, leaning on his car horn. —Light's green, idiot!

I slid down in the passenger seat and attempted to psychically communicate with the other drivers, trying my best to telepathically excuse my father's behavior. —*You should never know the pain of losing a child,* I thought to them.

—Pick a lane, bozo! my father shouted.

—Horse's ass!

—Step on it, pops!

—It's an old man, I said.

—He's not going to get any older, said my father, —if he doesn't get out of my goddamn lane.

—What's a miter joint?

—Not now.

Ten minutes later, we were in the lumber department at Rickel's and my father was whistling, loading a steel dolly with tall sheets of plywood, eight-foot-long two-by-fours and long, thin pieces of delicate oak trim he inspected closely before committing them to our cart. It was strange to think that this unholy pile of rough-hewn lumber was a holy ark; it seemed like plain old wood. And yet in a few weeks' time, this pile would be in our synagogue, and everyone would have to stand when the velvet curtain was drawn back ($3.29/sq. yd.), and they would have to pray when the red oak doors were opened ($6.50/sq. ft.), and at the end of the service, they would have to sing when they were closed on their heavy-duty decorative bronze hinges ($8.99 for a packet of two, including fasteners).

—*Where does the holy come from?* I wondered.

What if we'd come ten minutes later and someone else had taken these boards? What if they'd built a doghouse out of them, a tree house, an outhouse? What if we had come too early, and these were the outhouse boards? Is that why God had sent the old man to drive slowly in front of us? What if the holy ark boards were farther down in the pile?

I heard my father laughing. It was a sound I hadn't heard in a very long time.

—Well, yeah, he was joking with a Rickel's employee.

—I suppose if they're all wracked . . .

—. . . then maybe it's the straight ones that have the problem, said Mike, the Rickel's lumber associate.

—I'll tell you, my father said through the side of his mouth (this was the way he delivered his jokes—on the sly, as if he shouldn't, as if it were a sin), —if your prices were as good as your bullshit . . .

They laughed and laughed.

Suddenly I felt bad for my father. He was different from the other fathers. He wasn't a rabbi like Ephraim's or Shlomo's or Akiva's or Yechezkel's or Yoel's or Motty's or Dovid's or Shimon's, or a doctor like Ari's or Hillel's or Avi's or the other Avi's or Chaim's or Mordechai's. When he picked me up from yeshiva, he waited in his car at the back of the lot, by himself, away from the other fathers who stood conversing on the front steps of the school. On Sabbath, after services ended and my mother stood in front of the synagogue talking with her friends and neighbors, my father stood alone, by the side of the road at the far end of the synagogue's driveway, waiting for her with his hands in his pockets, singing traditional Yiddish Sabbath songs to which he didn't know the words.

—Yum, bum, biddy-biddy bum, he would sing. The Yiddish calm before the storm.

—I am not a thief, I would say.

—Knock it off. Go tell your mother we're leaving.

I would trudge across the parking lot, back to the synagogue, where my mother stood smiling and nodding, and I'd wait with her there, hiding in the crowd until my father gave up waiting and began to walk home alone. Then I would feel bad for him. I wondered what it would be like if nobody in your family wanted to walk home with you from synagogue. If they actually waited for you to leave so that they could walk home without you. If they silently hoped that this was the Sabbath you would get hit by a car on your way home from synagogue and that would be the end of that.

—*Goddamnit,* I would think, and hurry down the road to catch up with him.

My father and Mike the Rickel's lumber associate laughed and joked for another ten minutes before we left. As we pulled onto Route 59, a gray Ford Pinto with a Domino's Pizza sign on the roof swerved into our lane and cut us off. My father didn't say a word.

It wasn't as if Avrumi Mendlowitz had anything against me personally. It was just that he hadn't squeezed my balls yet.

—I'll get you soon, he'd say at lunch.

Everyone laughed.

Avrumi was in my fourth-grade class. Avrumi was big for his age, even if his age had been twenty-two. Every day, when yeshiva came to an end and we headed downstairs for the school buses, Avrumi would wait at the bottom of the stairwell and, spotting a suitable victim for the day, he would grab the boy, throw him to the ground, reach between his legs, and squeeze his balls. This made it difficult to tell on him, and Avrumi knew it. How do you say "balls" to a rabbi?

—Avrumi's beating people up, I said to Rabbi Goldfinger.

It was Monday afternoon, and Avrumi had chased me and my irresistible testes down the stairwell, through the hallway, and all the way to the front door before giving up on account of the heavy rabbinical presence.

—Who is he beating up? sighed Rabbi Goldfinger, and I was relieved; his exasperation seemed to indicate that he'd heard this complaint from others before.

—Everyone, I said.

—I don't see anyone looking beat up.

—Well, it's not exactly beating up . . .

Rabbi Goldfinger looked down at me. Behind his black horn-rimmed glasses and long black beard was a pair of warm, sensitive eyes beneath thick, expressive eyebrows. He put his hands on my shoulders, turned me in the direction of the waiting school buses, gave me a shove, and told me that if I knew what was good for me, I would stop trying to get other people in trouble.

Stupid Rabbi Goldfinger.

—Rabbi Goldfinger was right, said Ephraim the following Sunday afternoon. —You shouldn't tell on people. It's evil gossip. My father told me that if you speak evil gossip, then when you die, God hangs you by your tongue until it rips off and you die.

We were in my bedroom, playing Legos. Next door in the garage, work on the holy ark continued.

Ephraim and I competed for title of best student in the class, not including Yermiyahu Weider, who had a photographic memory, so it didn't really count. When Ephraim didn't get the highest grade in the class, he became worried. He wiggled his fingers. Ephraim's father was a rabbi. He was a tall man with a big black hat and a long black beard.

—A ninety-six? I heard him say to Ephraim one day after yeshiva. He shrugged with disappointment and handed the test back to his son. Ephraim wiggled his fingers.

—Bastard, said my father. He was in the garage, talking to his try square.

—It's not evil gossip, I said to Ephraim, —if it's true.

—But it wasn't true, said Ephraim. —You said he was beating people up.

—He grabs balls, I said. —He grabbed your balls last week.

—That's not beating up, said Ephraim.

It had been a week since the holy ark project began, and as the deadline grew nearer, my father's patience grew thinner, his temper more explosive.

—Who touched the goddamn thermostat? he bellowed. —Who took my vise grips? There are brownies missing! Those brownies were for *Shabbos*!

—Did it hurt? I asked Ephraim.

—What?

—Avrumi, I said.

Ephraim shrugged.

—Cocksucker, said my father.

—How come your father curses? Ephraim asked.

—I don't know, I said.

—My father says that the Sages say that *nivul peh* makes Jewish babies die.

Nivul peh meant using dirty language. In English, *nivul peh* meant "disgusting mouth."

—So? I responded. —I knew that. Of course I knew that.

I hadn't known that. Did my father know that? I had a disgusting-mouthed father and a dead brother; it was difficult to argue with the facts.

—So he shouldn't do it.

—So?

—So he shouldn't do it.

—So?

—So he shouldn't . . .

—Shalom! called my father. —Get in here.

—*Goddamnit,* I thought.

I could probably get better grades than Ephraim if I tried hard enough, but in the family lineage department, he had me flat-out beat. I may have been a Levite, but Ephraim was a Cohen, a priest, a genealogical royal flush, the only tribe tighter with God than the Levites. On top of that, Ephraim's father was a rabbi, and both of his grandfathers were rabbis. Kick-ass lineage. My lineage was in the garage next door, shouting obscenities at power tools; I'd be lucky if my lineage was wearing a yarmulke.

—Let's go, I said to Ephraim. Ephraim looked frightened.

—It's okay, I said.

Ephraim wiggled his fingers.

—Hold the end of this board up, said my father.

The good news was that my father was wearing his yarmulke. The bad news was that he wasn't wearing his shirt. I could tell the kind of work my father was doing by his particular degree of undress: he could make it through the light projects—patching drywall, touching up paint—with both his shirt and yarmulke staying on till the end. For finish carpentry—trimming, staining, clamping, gluing—he'd probably ditch the shirt about halfway through. If the work became heavy—framing, casework, landscaping—the yarmulke was gone, too. Over eighty-five degrees, he was down to his shorts and sandals, and we all hoped he would confine his labors to the backyard.

Ephraim wiggled his fingers and sheepishly made his way to the far corner of the garage. The hair on my father's chest was covered with sawdust, and his stomach hung heavily over his weary black belt. I'd been to Ephraim's house dozens of times, and never once saw his father without his shirt on. I'd never seen him without his suit jacket on. One time his shoelace was untied, but that was an accident, and after he tied it, he told me what the Sages say about he who is so involved with the words of the Torah that he forsakes his own appearance.

It was something positive.

—How come you never have friends over? my mother would sometimes ask. —You're such a loner.

My father hiked up his pants and brushed the sawdust off his chest. I lifted the end of the board over my head to bring it level with the table of the saw, and my father turned on the power. Ephraim, unaccustomed to the sound of the saw, stood in the driveway with his fingers in his ears.

—Easy! shouted my father over the screaming of the saw. —Higher! That's it! Easy!

My father sneered through the sawdust; the saw shuddered, the board shook. Angry splinters pushed into my hands as I tried to control the violent side-to-side movements I knew would burn the edges of the board. When the board had finally made it through the blade, my father pulled off his goggles and switched off the saw. Ephraim pulled his fingers out of his ears. My father turned the board onto its side and inspected the curved black marks that rippled down its side.

—Son of a bitch, he said.

Ephraim jammed his fingers back in his ears.

—What's a biscuit joiner? I asked.

—Not now, said my father.

We went back inside, and Ephraim phoned his mother. We took my Steve Austin doll out to the front yard and waited for her.

—Who's that? asked Ephraim.

—Steve Austin, I said.

The Six Million Dollar Man was my favorite show. I'd sent away for Steve Austin's autograph weeks ago, but it still hadn't arrived.

—You're not supposed to watch TV, said Ephraim. —My father says it's a tool of the evil inclination.

—I know, I said.

—How come your father has so many tools? Ephraim asked.

—He builds things, I said.

—Why?

—Because he likes to.

—Why?

—I don't know, I said. —It's cool.

—No, it isn't.

—Yes, it is.

—My father says anything that takes away time from serving God is wrong, said Ephraim.

—He's building a holy ark, you stupid idiot.

That shut him up for a little while, until my father walked by without his yarmulke. That was good news for the project—it meant he'd moved on to the heavier casement work—but bad news for me.

—How come your father isn't wearing a yarmulke? Ephraim asked.

—I don't know, I said.

—My father says that if you take four steps without your yarmulke, it's like saying that you're not scared of God.

—I know.

—So how come he doesn't wear one?

—I don't know.

—Is he scared of God?

—I don't know.

—He should be.

—I know.

My Levite blood was beginning to boil.

—Why does he curse?

—I don't know.

—He shouldn't.

—I know.

Cocksucker.

My mother's brother was a famous rabbi. His name was Uncle Nathan. Her other brother was also a famous rabbi. His name was Uncle Mendel. Uncle Nathan lived in New York, and Uncle Mendel lived in Los Angeles. They both had the same goatees. They both wrote books. Uncle Nathan was also a doctor. Sometimes he called himself Rabbi Doctor and sometimes he called himself Doctor Rabbi. Uncle Mendel wasn't a doctor, but he was the rabbi of a very big synagogue in Los Angeles.

—You know who goes to my synagogue? he would say when he came to visit. —Alan Alda.

—Wow! my mother would say.

I didn't know who Alan Alda was.

—From the television, she would add. —You know. You love that show.

—Big donor, my uncle would say.

With only one Sunday left to finish the ark, my mother made plans for us to go see Uncle Nathan in Manhattan.

My father leaned on the car horn, and shouted at the other cars.

—Jackass! he called.

—Horse's ass!

—Look at this shithead, will you? Will you look at this shithead?

—How do they make Sheetrock? I asked.

—I hate this goddamned city, muttered my father.

—Does a dado blade do the same thing as a router? Because if they do, then how do you know which—

—Not now, he said.

I never felt comfortable at my uncle's apartment, and neither, it seemed to me, did my father. Uncle Nathan had recently been made president of one of the biggest yeshivas in the country. There was a man at the front of his apartment building who opened the door for you; another man inside the lobby who asked your name and then phoned upstairs and said, "The Auslanders are here. . . . Very good"; and a man who sat in the old-fashioned elevator and closed the metal gates and turned a big handle that made the elevator go up and down. My uncle had a maid, and a limo, and a driver. All of them were black. His apartment had three floors. All of them were marble. It was no Rickel's.

—That's called a triplex! my mother said to us as we rode up the elevator to my uncle's apartment.

The Levite inside me began to seethe. What was the big deal, anyway? So he was a rabbi? So Ephraim's father was a rabbi? So what? What did they actually do, anyway? All I ever saw my uncle do was shake hands. My father built tables. He built decks.

The elevator man smiled at us.

—I've never even *seen* the inside of a triplex, my mother said to my father. —Have you?

—Yum, bum, biddy-biddy bum, he said.

My aunt met us at the door.

—You know who lives there? she whispered, pointing to the apartment door across the way. —Harrison Ford.

—Wow, said my mother. —The movie star?

My aunt nodded.

—Luke Skywalker, she said.

He was Han Solo.

—Did you see that movie? my mother asked me.

I wondered if Harrison Ford met his guests at the door. *You know who lives there, Chewbacca? A rabbi.*

—No, I lied.

—Of course you did, said my mother.

I shrugged. My aunt invited us into the kitchen to get something to eat.

—Boy, said my mother, you could fit three of our kitchens in here, couldn't you, Shal?

My mother stayed in the three-kitchen kitchen with my aunt, while I trudged behind my father into the den. The dark walls were lined with shelves, heavy with books. In the corner was a grand piano nobody ever played, and on the table in front of the couch (—*Settee,* my mother whispered) was a pile of books that nobody ever read. All of them were about Israel. One was about art. It was called *Art in Israel.* My father sat on the couch, put his hands behind his head and affected a terribly unconvincing air of ease.

—Yum, bum, biddy-biddy bum, he said.

After what seemed like hours, the door to my uncle's study opened and a man in a black hat and suit emerged. My uncle followed after him, slapping him on the back and handing him his coat. They were both smoking cigars, and they stood in the foyer shaking hands. My father stood up, straightened his tie, and tucked in his shirt, but my uncle took the man by the shoulder, turned him away, and led him past us to the front door, where they shook hands again as the man left.

My father clasped his hands behind his back, walked to the bookshelf, and looked closely at *The Teachings of Rabbi Soloveitchik,* as if that were the reason he had stood up in the first place.

—Yum, bum, biddy-biddy bum, he said.

Behind my father's back, my brother pointed at him and silently laughed.

—Big donor, my uncle said to my mother when he came into the den. He shook my father's hand. He shook my brother's hand. He shook my hand. He sat down.

—So, he said to my father, —what's new with you?

I waited for someone to mention the ark.

—What's new with *us*? My mother laughed. Then, with great import: —Tell me, Nathan, how are things at the yeshiva?

—Well, my uncle began.

It would be some time before he finished.

And the Levites did as Moses commanded, and that day about three thousand of the people died.

I felt bad for my father. I wondered what it would feel like to be great at something nobody thought was all that great. To be good with your hands in a world that judged people by their heads. To be a creator in a world that kneeled before quibblers, beggars, and handshakers. I was beginning to want to flood the Earth myself.

I wanted to leave.

I wanted to go to Rickel's.

—You know who was here yesterday? said my uncle. —Herman Wouk.

Cocksucker.

—The author? asked my mother.

It was almost eleven o'clock by the time we left, and well past midnight when we arrived back in Monsey. My father opened the garage doors, took off his shirt, and went back to work.

—He's pretty special, my mother said as we walked into the house.

I nodded.

—And that apartment of his, she continued. —I mean, did you ever?

The next week my father went to the synagogue without me and installed the holy ark that I'd helped him build. The day that he did, Avrumi Mendlowitz grabbed my balls.

My guard was down. Competing with Ephraim in class every day, running home to check the mail to see if Steve Austin had replied to my letter, coming up with endless woodworking questions to keep my father from killing my brother, and working till late on the holy ark—sanding, staining, gluing, nailing—something had to give.

The deadline for the holy ark was Friday, and the nearer it drew, the worse my father became. Monday night he threw my brother out of the house and told him never to come back. My mother intervened and said, —Please, but my brother grabbed his backpack and ran out the back door. My mother drove around for hours looking for him.

I paced the hall, worried, and looked up at the photograph of Jeffie.

—Cocksucker, I said.

Wednesday night my father couldn't find his tack hammer.

—Your no-good brother comes in here, he said through clenched teeth, —and just takes, takes, takes.

He rolled up his sleeves, started to make his way into the house.

—Takes, takes, takes, he growled.

—How do they make sandpaper? I called after him. —What's a nailset? Should I use wood glue or epoxy?

—Gotcha, said Avrumi.

It was the end of the day. My mind was busy with Steve Austin and rabbit joints, and without thinking, I took the main stairs with all the other students. Avrumi was waiting for me at the bottom.

He threw me on the ground, and lay on top of me. His breath smelled of fish cakes and milk, and he grunted as he put his hand between my legs and squeezed.

—Cocksucker, I said.

Everyone gasped.

—Disgusting mouth! shouted Avrumi, pointing an accusatory finger at me with his left hand. —Disgusting mouth! Disgusting mouth! You're going to hang by your tongue!

His right hand was still crushing my balls.

The garage doors were open when I came home. The ark was gone.

—Where's the ark? I asked my mother.

—How should I know? she said.

—Where's Dad? I asked.

—Oh, that's right, she said. —He took the ark to the synagogue.

—Oh.

—What's wrong?

I shrugged.

—Did something happen at school?

I shrugged.

—I have something that will cheer you up.

She handed me a large white envelope. It was addressed to My Biggest Fan. I tore the envelope open and pulled out a large color photograph of Steve Austin. There was handwriting across the bottom of the photo.

For Sharon, it read. *Love, Lee Majors.*

—Who's Sharon? I asked my mother.

She shrugged.

—Who's Lee Majors? I asked.

She shrugged.

—They probably got your name wrong, she said.

—Which name? I asked. —Sharon or Lee Majors?

—Sharon. Lee Majors is the actor.

—What actor?

—The actor that plays Steve Whatever His Name Is.

—But I didn't want an actor's signature. I wanted Steve Austin's signature.

—Please, said my mother.

Friday afternoons, before yeshiva closed for the weekend, the hallways filled with students, a tempestuous sea of white shirts and black pants, as we all made our way to the synagogue for the weekly lecture from Rabbi Goldfinger, our principal, on the importance of Sabbath. That Friday, as we made our way to the synagogue, the door to Rabbi Goldfinger's office was open, a rare occurrence, and we stopped to look inside.

Rabbi Goldfinger was sitting behind his desk, facing both Avrumi and a thick-bearded giant wearing a dark blue suit and a gray wide-brimmed fedora.

—Avrumi's father, someone whispered.

Avrumi had been crying. Rabbi Goldfinger was talking,

but we couldn't hear what he was saying. He saw us watching him, but he didn't close the door. He continued speaking to Avrumi's father, who shook his head and rubbed his eyes with the thumb and forefinger of his hand before suddenly pulling his arm back and smacking Avrumi so hard on his bottom that Avrumi was pushed into the sharp corner of Rabbi Goldfinger's desk. Avrumi spun around, holding his hands on his bottom, and noticed us watching from the door. He tried to make a funny face, but his father lifted his hand over his head as if to strike him again, and Avrumi flinched. Rabbi Goldfinger sagely twisted his beard and fixed his stare on those of us watching from the doorway.

—No *aveiras*? Rabbi Goldfinger shouted at us. —Somebody there has no *aveiras*?

We turned and walked away.

Aveiras are sins.

The ark was magnificent.

My father had designed the case so that when the doors were opened, there'd be no rail down the center to disrupt the view of the holy scrolls. In tall, golden Hebrew letters across the top of the ark, my father had spelled out the biblical passage "Know Before Whom You Stand," and in those golden letters were caught and reflected the flickering lights of the *ner tamid,* or eternal candle, which hung, forever lit, over the cantor's podium. A deep blue velvet curtain adorned the front, trimmed in silver and golden piping, and in the center, where the two halves of the curtain met, stood two golden lions beside the two tablets of the Ten Commandments. It still didn't seem holy to me: I was afraid for my father, worried that someone would discover its non-holiness and have him start over. —*Hey,* they would shout, —*this is just lumber!*—but it was beautiful, and it filled the wall, and it made Rabbi Blonsky, sitting beside it in his new leather chair, seem like a child, like a little boy playing dress-up in a wise man's clothes.

That day, my father sang more loudly than I had ever heard him before. He joked with Dr. Kaplan. He laughed with Dr. Becker. He shook hands, vigorously, with Dr. Malinowitz. He seemed happy, as he was at Rickel's, though he was careful not to make any hardware jokes. Finally, the time for the reading of the Torah arrived, and the entire congregation rose to their feet. Silence filled the synagogue as God's Holy Spirit rested on the ark my father had built. The cantor threw back his head and called out the blessings on the Torah. —Amen, said the congregation. Then he moved to the ark, and pulled aside the heavy blue curtain. Everyone prayed aloud, singing and welcoming both the new Torah and the holy ark in which it rested. The cantor approached the doors, grabbed the handle, and pulled.

Nothing.

He pulled again.

Nothing.

He pulled a third time, harder, so hard that his prayer shawl slipped from his shoulder and he had to catch his yarmulke with his other hand. Rabbi Blonsky hurried over and tried his luck, but the door refused to open. He held his yarmulke on his head with one hand and tried again, more forcefully, with the other. The ark tipped slightly forward.

—Whoa! shouted a few of the men in the front row, shuffling backward out of harm's way.

Rabbi Blonsky turned to face the congregation and shrugged before raising his hand above his head and twisting it left and right, as if opening a lock. *Is there a key to this damn thing?* he mimed.

People started to laugh.

My father's face turned red and he began motioning to Rabbi Blonsky to pull the doors from the top. In order to give an unobstructed view of the Torahs, there could be no center rail, and because there could be no center rail, the door latches had to be located at the tops of the doors. Rabbi Blonsky saw my father motioning, but thought he was indicating that the key was on top of the ark, and he began feeling around on top of the ark for a key that wasn't there to a lock that didn't exist.

Dr. Frankel laughed. Dr. Eisenberg shrugged and smiled. My father continued motioning for them to pull from the top of the doors while my brother nudged me and rolled his eyes. Finally, the cantor reached up, pulled on the corner, and the door swung open. A few people clapped.

—Mazel tov, called Mr. Pomerantz.

—*Cocksucker,* I thought.

The cantor began singing again, draped his prayer shawl

back over his shoulder, and opened wide the ark's second door.

You really *could* see all the scrolls.

When the services ended, my father, instead of heading down the parking lot away from the crowd, stood with the rest of the congregation just outside the front doors. I stood with him, waiting for my mother to make her way outside. My father stood with his head up, his hands behind his back. He seemed proud. He wished a good *Shabbos* to some of our neighbors, who, after some initial surprise, returned the greeting and moved on, never saying a word about the ark. Soon my mother appeared with her old friend Mrs. Pleeter.

—You can't imagine, my mother was saying, —the amount of work.

Mrs. Pleeter was nodding as the two of them came over.

—You must be very proud, she said to me.

I dug my hands into my pockets and shrugged. My father did the same. Mrs. Pleeter leaned over and straightened my tie.

—Well, you should be, she said. —You have a very famous uncle, did you know that?

My mother beamed.

—Actually, she corrected Mrs. Pleeter, —he has *two* famous uncles.

—Yum, bum, biddy-biddy bum, said my father.

The Beckers said, —*Gut Shabbos,* and so did the Baums and the Frankels, but no one had yet mentioned the ark.

Finally, Mr. Pomerantz came over, shook my father's hand, and said, —Beautiful job. Took you a while?

My father smiled and shrugged. —*Nisht geferlach,* he said in Yiddish. Not so bad.

—The doors, continued Mr. Pomerantz with a smile. —Maybe the edges need a *shtickel* sanding?

My father smiled back. —I'll sand your edges, he said through his teeth.

Mrs. Borgen came outside, kissed my mother on the cheek, and said how much she enjoyed my uncle's book. The book was called *A Bed of Roses.* It was a guide to having a happy marriage.

—Yum, bum, biddy-biddy bum, said my father.

He began to make his way to the end of the synagogue's driveway.

—He's going, I said to my mother.

—Of all my brother's books, my mother was saying to Mrs. Borgen, —that one really is my favorite.

—He's going . . .

—Okay, said my mother, patting me on the back. —Go. Go.

Goddamnit, I thought.

We walked a long way without saying a word.

—What kind of a stupid rabbi can't open a door? I finally said.

—Watch your mouth, he said.

—What did I say?

—Just watch it.

—Is oak stronger than maple?

We walked the rest of the way in silence.

Something happened. Or maybe nothing happened. Maybe everything just seems better when you're four years old. The Levite in me shrugged and didn't care.

Avrumi was a different boy on Monday morning. He paid attention during class, and if he didn't always have the answers, he also wasn't shooting spitballs and drawing cartoons in the margins of his Talmud. Outside class, though, he seemed defeated. He walked through the halls by himself, his head down and his hands in his pockets. At lunch, he sat alone. Afterward, we had a surprise Bible test. Ephraim got a ninety-eight and I got a ninety-six. Because we had received the two highest scores, Rabbi Napier had us hand back the tests to the rest of the students. As I handed Avrumi his test, I noticed he had managed only a sixty-eight.

Suddenly I felt bad for Avrumi. Maybe he was ashamed of his poor test scores. Maybe the only thing anyone ever gave him credit for was his size and strength. Maybe he was attacking other boys in the stairwell because it was all that was expected of him.

I stopped Avrumi on his way to the bus.

—That was a hard test, I said.

Avrumi looked down at me and let his backpack slip from his shoulder.

—I mean, even Yermiyahu only got a ninety-two, I said. —And he has a photographic memory . . .

Avrumi pushed me onto the ground, fell on top of me and squeezed my balls.

—Yeahhhh . . . he grunted, his sour breath filling my nostrils, his face only inches from mine. —Yeahhhh . . .

Rabbi Napier told us that after building his ark, all Noah had to do was pray for the people of the world—just once— and God would have saved them all. But Noah didn't pray.

Maybe he was tired of trying to save them.

Maybe he wanted to watch them all drown.

Now the Earth was corrupt before God and full of violence. . . . And God said to Noah, "I am going to put an end to all flesh, for the Earth is filled with violence because of them, and I am surely going to destroy them with the Earth."

I lay there on my back, pinned to the ground beneath the dull, grunting heap of Avrumi as he continued his assault, and I looked up—past his pasty cheek, past his oily *peyis,* past his maroon-and-silver yarmulke, past the flat gray roof of the brown brick yeshiva building to the blackening sky above, where great, grave clouds quietly assembled, cracking their knuckles, punching their palms, and waiting. It looked, I hoped, like rain.

5.

*S*top me if you've heard this joke before:

—Something's wrong, said Orli.

I could tell through the phone that she had been crying. —What, I asked, —what is it?

I could hear her trying to catch her breath. She was panicking. Me, I'm a rock.

—WHAT, already, fuck, what, Orli, what's going on, what is it, don't just call me three months pregnant crying and not . . . WHAT?

The tests came back, she told me. Something was wrong with the baby.

—*You fucking Fuck,* I said to God. —*You fucking, fucking Fuck.*

I believe in a personal God; everything I do, He takes personally. Things don't just happen.

—God speaks to everyone, every day, said my teachers. —But you have to listen.

—Why me? my mother would cry as she paid the bills or

cooked the dinners or paid for the clothes or came home from the dentist. —I must have done something, she would say. —I don't know what, but I must have done something.

I once knew a rabbi who had been born with a mild form of cerebral palsy. His right leg was locked straight at the knee, his right arm was locked bent at the elbow. He was hard of hearing. His eyesight was going. His house had burned down. His eldest child had taken ill and died. —God is telling me something, he used to say with a smile. —He's telling me I have a great reward in the next life!

There's an old joke about a deaf, one-eyed crippled dog that ends the same exact way: *Answers to the name of Lucky.*

I wonder sometimes if he—and I—suffer from a metaphysical form of Stockholm syndrome. Held captive by this Man for thousands of years, we now praise Him, defend Him, excuse Him, sometimes kill for Him, an army of Squeaky Frommes swearing allegiance to their Charlie in the sky. My relationship with God has been an endless cycle not of the celebrated "faith followed by doubt," but of appeasement followed by revolt; placation followed by indifference; please, please, please, followed by fuck it, fuck You, fuck off. I do not keep Sabbath or pray three times a day or wait six hours between eating meat and milk. The people who raised me will say that I am not religious. They are mistaken. What I am not is *observant.* But I am painfully, cripplingly, incurably, miserably religious, and I have watched lately, dumbfounded and distraught, as around the world, more and more people seem to be finding Gods, each one more hateful and bloodthirsty than the next, as I'm doing my best to lose Him. I'm failing miserably.

I believe in God.

It's been a real problem for me.

I have very little sympathy for veal.

According to the website NoVeal.org, *Young calves are taken from their mothers and chained by the neck in crates measuring just two feet wide. They cannot turn around, stretch their limbs, or even lie down comfortably.* Like a yeshiva—or a madrasa, or a Catholic school. Except for the "taken from their mother" bit, the lucky little calves; my mother put me in the box and made it very clear that her love was conditional upon my remaining in the box. To make matters better, nobody is standing outside the veal's crate telling him that there is a some sort of Cow Almighty in the sky, and that Cow Almighty commands the veal to stay in that box, and that, moreover, the constraining box he finds himself in is a gift—a gift from Cow Almighty because veal are Cow's chosen cattle, and if veal even thinks about leaving the box, or questioning the box, or even complaining about the box, well, Cow help him.

I've been in a mini-revolt phase lately. I have been doing my work, and writing my stories with my regard for God and His Department of Ironic Punishmentation temporarily suspended. I sat down in my office that morning with a coffee in my hand and a chip on my shoulder. —*Blow me, O Lord,* I thought as I started up my laptop. —*Do Your worst.*

And then Orli called.

—What tests? I asked her. —Who called you, what are you . . . What tests?

They were called alpha-fetoprotein tests, and combined with an enzyme/hormone test, they tell you what the chances are that your baby has Down's syndrome. The nurse had phoned that morning, just after I'd left, and told her that the chance our baby had Down's syndrome was 1 in 20. Normal was 1 in 270.

Orli was crying.

—I don't understand, I said.

Someone has this job? Someone wakes up, brushes her teeth, picks up some coffee and then spends the day calling around, telling people that their unborn children have Down's syndrome? Over the *phone*? What kind of a sick fucking job is this? How do you get this job? Pull all the legs off a spider and drop it in a cup? *Nice. We especially like how you left the last leg on so it would think it had a chance. Good stuff. Can you start Monday?*

I didn't understand.

—I don't understand.

And calm down. And just calm down. And they could be wrong, and I'm coming home, and are you crying, and I'm okay, I'll be home in a few minutes and what are we going to do, and just CALM DOWN and don't shout at me and I'm sorry and I love you and I love you and I love you and it's going to be okay.

You fuck, God. You fucking, fucking Fuck.

I pulled on my coat, grabbed my keys, threw my laptop into my bag, ran out of my office, climbed into my truck, closed the door, started the engine, took my laptop out of my bag, deleted all the God stories I'd been working on (*Are you sure?* the computer asked. *You cannot undo this action.* I was sure), closed my laptop, put it in my bag, put the truck in gear, and floored it.

Orli's mother is Egyptian. Her father is Bukharan. Their house is in London, but for most of the year they reside in the sixteenth century. Her relationship with them is cordial, but she is not about to phone them for advice, medical or otherwise. The phone would ring in their kitchen, her father would try to answer the toaster, and her mother would stand in the doorway and scowl.

—Seendome? her father would ask. —What is this seendome?

—Syndrome, Orli would shout into the phone. —Syndrome! Down's! Syndrome!

—Down, yes. What is down?

As for me, my mother has a son named Shalom that she loves dearly, but he isn't me or, more accurately, I'm not him. He is married with many children, and he lives next door to her, in a proper *Yiddishe* community, and he keeps the Sabbath and he calls it *Shabbos,* and he phones her before *Shabbos* and wishes her *Gutten Shabbos,* and he meets her in synagogue on *Shabbos* and they walk home together on

Shabbos, and he phones her after *Shabbos* and wishes her a good week and he calls it a *gut voch,* and all the myriad conditions of her love are blissfully met. She has been the victim of some cosmic bait-and-switch, and she has spent the years since I have dared to become myself looking for the receipt. —*This,* she says as she pats her pockets and looks through her coat, —*is not what I purchased.*

With no one else to go to for answers, we went to Google. Here's the punch line:

—Whoopsie, said the nurse.

A mistake.

Orli caught it herself a few sleepless nights later, based on some information she had found online: the alpha-feto test is based on the fetus's age, and someone, in our case, had entered the wrong date of conception. Someone had forgotten to carry the 1. Our chances of having a baby with Down's syndrome were actually 1 in 766.

Good one, God.

—What did they say? I asked.

—They said I was right.

—Did they apologize?

—No. Shal . . .

—Was it the same one? I asked.

—The same what?

—The same nurse that called to tell you he was Down's?

—What's the difference?

—What's the difference?

—What's the difference?

—I need to know how many nurses to kill, that's the difference. Is it one or two?

I pictured a blue-haired, Yoda-shaped doctor's assistant wedged behind her desk, surrounded by troll dolls, snow globes and lipstick-stained coffee cups, counting days since conception on the knuckles of her chubby little fist. *Thirty days has November, April, May . . . no, wait . . . Thirty days . . . hang on now . . .*

And then we hugged, and we held each other and we stayed like that for a while until the dogs started whining and we took them up the mountain for a hike.

—How's the book coming? asked Orli.

—Not so good, I said.

I have very little sympathy for veal.

6.

*I*t all started with a Slim Jim.

I was nine years old. It was a Sunday afternoon in June, and I was at the Ramapo town pool with my mother and her usual bag of warm fruit, cold shnitzel, kosher cookies, and a copy of *The Jewish Press*. The pool was my escape, a cool, azure, rabbi-free rectangle with two smaller rectangles at either end, one for the shallow end and one for the deep. Here you could relax, take off your *tzitzis,* stuff your yarmulke in your flip-flops and forget about God for a while. Boys did cannonballs off the high dive, shouting loudly as they leaped; girls did underwater handstands, legs glistening in the sunlight as their girlfriends squealed and cheered them on. The black kids played basketball, the white kids played Frisbee, and the ultra-Orthodox stayed home. Swimming, unless boys and girls were separated, was forbidden, but it was one of my parents' few concessions to their happiness in this world over their eternal rewards in the next.

Someone I named Kevin called out —*Marco!*; someone I named Johnny called out —*Polo!*; and a tall, skinny guy with shoulder-length blond hair—I named him Vinnie—walked toward us with a girl I named Tiffany. She was taller than Vinnie, her hair even longer and blonder. Her swimsuit was tiny, nothing more than a pair of miniature white yarmulkes tied to the tips of her breasts and a shiny white *hamentash* wedged between her legs. Vinnie's arm was draped around Tiffany's shoulder; Tiffany's hand was wedged into the back pocket of his cut-off denim shorts. As they walked toward us, the hair on the tops of their heads bounced up and down, and as they walked past, the hair on the back of their heads bounced left and right. Their hair seemed happy. They seemed happy. Vinnie was wearing a long silver necklace, basketball sneakers without laces, and a T-shirt that read "Iron Maiden" on the front. On the back, a naked lady was licking a tall glistening sword.

My hair was short.

My shoes were penny loafers.

My T-shirt read "We Want the Messiah Now."

—*A feineh mensch,* my mother muttered sarcastically in Yiddish as they walked away. A fine young man.

The air that day was still, and I was twisting uncomfortably in my lounge chair, trying to get out from beneath the furious gaze of the sun above. Suddenly, as if from nowhere, a breeze drifted by, and something wonderful rode upon that breeze, something sweet and sharp, foul and fantastic all at the same time, something that made my nostrils open and my mouth water. I rose and lifted my nose into the air, trying to follow that scent to the place from whence it came, and then a second breeze joined the first; together they filled my nose with the irresistible smell of *traif* (non-kosher) meat that was grilling at the Snack Shack on the far side of the pool.

—Can I have a dollar? I asked my mother.

—There are some apples in my bag, she answered from behind her *Jewish Press*. "PLO Promises More Attacks," the headline promised.

—But I want a soda.

She sighed deeply, handed me her wallet, and told me to take a dollar. I took two and ran off.

—Yarmulke! she shouted.

I ran back, grabbed my yarmulke from her outstretched hand, stuffed it into the waistband of my bathing suit, and hurried off to join Vinn and Tiff at the Snack Shack.

—I'll have a Coke, I said to the man behind the counter.

—Anything else?

Vinnie stood beside me, piling his pig dog high with sauerkraut and thin-cut pickles. I stared, openmouthed, as he flipped his hair back, cleared a path to his mouth, and took a bite. It was as if he'd never even heard of Leviticus 11:7.

—What's the matter, kid? asked Vinnie. —Never seen a dude eat a dog before?

It was a pig I'd never seen a dude eat before.

—Well, kid? asked the Snack Shack man. —What's it going to be?

When Rabbi Shimon bar Yochai was hiding in a cave from the Romans, God spoke to him, and Rabbi Shimon bar Yochai wrote down everything God said to him. The name of the book of the things that God told him is the Zohar, and it is one of the most sacred books in all of Judaism. This is what Rabbi Shimon bar Yochai said that God said about someone who eats non-kosher: *God loathes him in this world and He tortures him in the next.*

—I don't have all day, kid, said the Snack Shack man. —Anything else?

—One of those, I said, pointing to a white plastic bucket sitting on the edge of the counter.

—A Slim Jim? he asked.

I nodded.

My heart raced as the Snack Shack man reached over and pulled a Slim Jim from the bucket. I'd seen Slim Jims before, at the local deli, and had marveled at them from afar.

—Imagine that, I'd thought. —A *stick* of *meat*!

Kosher meat is very complicated. Animals without split hooves are forbidden. Animals that don't chew their cud are forbidden. Unless the animals are slaughtered in a very specific way, they are forbidden. Someone has to verify that the animal was slaughtered in a very specific way, and there has to be a mark on the package saying, "This meat has been slaughtered in a very specific way." If the package does not have that mark, it is forbidden.

A stick. Of meat! Anytime you wanted, wherever you wanted. *Give me a comic book, a bottle of milk, and a stick of meat.* What a life.

—Cheese or regular? the Snack Shack man asked.

What was the big deal, anyway? With their bright red

and yellow wrappers, Slim Jims seemed more like candy than a forbidden food. Had God even seen these things? How could He get so worked up about *candy*? He was going to torture a kid because of *candy*? It wasn't as if I'd ordered a hot dog. I wasn't completely insane. Hot dogs were the deep end of the non-kosher pool; I was trying to avoid God loathing me completely in this world, and hoped if I started at the shallow end, with a Slim Jim, He might just vaguely dislike me, or generally prefer the company of others.

—Well? asked the Snack Shack man.

Traif was more than just a word for forbidden food. *Traif* meant someone or something was disgusting, vile, foul, immoral, twisted, loathsome. Going to movies was *traif*, watching televison was *traif*. New York City was *traif*. Woody Allen was *traif*. My friend Tzvi had an older brother who didn't wear a yarmulke and was dating a non-Jewish girl. Tzvi's brother was very *traif*. But nothing—nothing— was more *traif* than actually eating *traif*.

—Come on, kid, the Snack Shack man said. —Cheese or regular?

There was no sin in just *buying* it, was there? I could always throw it out. It's not like I *had* to eat it. I mean, if just buying something that might be used to commit a sin was in itself a sin, then you probably couldn't buy a car because you might drive it on Sabbath, right? But Rabbi Kahn had a car; my parents had two cars. Rabbi Shimon bar Yochai prob- ably had a car.

—Cheese it is, said the Snack Shack man.

Eating non-kosher meat was bad enough; if I ate it combined with non-kosher cheese, God would never let me out of the pool alive. He'd bash my head on the diving board. He'd give me a cramp in the deep end, whether I waited a half hour before swimming or not. Did one have to wait longer after eating traif? I wondered. Maybe the body didn't even register it as food, and I wouldn't have to wait at all? What a life. Either way, He'd find a way to drown me. Then He'd drown my mother. She might even be dead already.

—Regular, I said. —Please, please, regular.

What was I doing? What was wrong with me? Why couldn't I be like the other boys? My friends were all kosher. My school was kosher. My brother and sister were kosher. We went to kosher restaurants. We shopped in kosher stores. Our toothpaste was kosher. Our hand soap was kosher. Our dishwashing liquid was kosher. We had separate sinks, one for meat and one for dairy. We had separate meat and dairy dishes, separate meat and dairy pots, separate meat and dairy utensils. If a dairy utensil even brushed against a meat utensil, my mother would shout and hurry to the living room where she would bury them both in the houseplant by the window. Only the ends of the handles would be visible above the soil, and there they would remain, their handles sticking up in shame, until a few days later, when they would somehow be kosher again.

I was about to cross a line that nobody I knew had ever crossed, a line Rabbi Shimon bar Yochai said that God said could never be uncrossed. —*He who eats forbidden foods,*

God said to Rabbi Shimon bar Yochai, —*can never be puri-fied.* Once you go Snack Shack, you never go back.

My mouth went dry. My hands shook. I looked to Vin-nie for a little support in my time of need, but he was busy feeding his hot dog to Tiffany. She took a bite, chewed, and wasn't killed—smiled, in fact, as mustard ran down her chin and dripped onto the crucifix hanging from her neck. Vin-nie leaned over and licked it off.

Jesus Christ.

—Make it two, I said to the Snack Shack man.

—Two it is, he said.

I was snowballing. One minute more and I'd be nose-deep in a large beef chili and a plate of Super Nachos.

—Two seventy-five, the Snack Shack man said.

I stood up on my tiptoes and handed him my mother's money, breaking her heart, the law, and six thousand years of tradition in a single moment.

—You're seventy-five cents short, he said.

This was God; this was God Himself, intervening in my behalf, giving me one last chance to pull myself back from the brink of . . .

—Skip the soda, I said.

I grabbed my Slim Jims and sat down at a nearby picnic table. I tore one open and held it up to my nose, inhaling deeply as I'd seen my grandfather do when he opened a fresh jar of herring. So this was what it was like, I thought. This was what it was like to be one of them—the people who drove by us as we walked to synagogue on Saturday, the people who watched TV on Friday night, the people who could eat sticks of meat, who lived with Ramapo-pool-type freedom every blessed day of their un-Chosen lives. I closed my eyes, took a deep breath, and shoved as much of the Slim Jim into my mouth as I could, coiling it up inside my mouth like a pig-flavored garden hose, forcing the last few reddish brown inches with the tips of my impure, trembling fingers as I tried in vain to squeeze my lips shut.

—Hungry? asked Vinnie.

I shrugged and tried to smile, but my eyes had filled with tears as my nostrils filled with the stench of a thousand oven-smoked swine. I couldn't breathe. Thick, brown ooze sludged out of the corner of my mouth and crept down my chin. It dripped onto my shirt, and landed with a hideous splat on the M of the word "Messiah."

Vinnie smiled.

Tiffany winced.

My stomach heaved. I ran for the nearest trash can, a black metal drum swarming with bees and flies and stink, and I threw myself over the side.

—Yuck, I heard Tiffany whine. —Gross, kid.

Yellow jackets, sent by God to punish me, circled my head but I hung there for a few moments longer, trying to catch my breath and hoping that eventually everyone would look away. When I finally straightened up, Tiff and Vinn were staring at me.

I smiled and tried to be cool, folding my arms across my

chest and leaning nonchalantly against the bin. Something shifted inside my trunks. My yarmulke dropped out and fell to the floor.

Tiffany rolled her eyes.

Vinnie smiled and nodded.

—Jimmies, he said with a knowing shake of his head. —You can't fight the Jimmies.

I was back at the Snack Shack one week later, and back again many times throughout that summer. Regular Slim Jims, spicy Slim Jims, cheese-flavored Slim Jims. One nearly disastrous afternoon, I went there with my older sister, who wanted a Coke and a bag of peanuts.

—Jimmy? asked the Snack Shack man.

—Who's Jimmy? she asked.

—How should I know? I said.

I lived in constant fear of being caught. My friends at yeshiva would never understand. I'd be lucky if they ever spoke to me again. If their parents found out I was *traif,* they would forbid their children from being my friend. My rabbis would pray for my forgiveness. My father would throw me out of the house. And my mother? My mother would bury me in the dirt until I was kosher again.

I spent my allowance on Three Musketeers and ate them in hiding at the top of a pine tree in the woods behind our house. I hid Mallow Cups in my sock drawer. I hid Nacho Cheese Doritos in my underwear drawer. I rode my bike to the nearby convenience mart, bought a couple of Moon

Pies, and rode back, terrified the whole way that I would get hit by a car, die, and my mother would find them in my pocket. That would be so God.

I tried to convince myself it was just a phase. *I can stop at any time.* I tried to put it out of my mind, tried stuffing myself with challah and kasha, but it was no use. At the supermarket, I would trudge alongside my mother through aisle after aisle of the finless, the scaleless, the split-hoofless, past row after row of things made with pig, or pig fat, or gelatin, trying my very best to convince her they were kosher.

—How about Franken Berry? I asked.

—It's not kosher.

—But it has a K on it.

—K isn't kosher. It has to have an OK, or an OU.

—What about a TM? Franken Berry has a TM.

—That's a trademark symbol.

—How about an OC?

—That's a copyright symbol.

—How about Lucky Charms, can we get Lucky Charms?

—No.

—Why not?

—They're *traif,* she would say.

—What's *traif* about them?

—They've got marshmallows in them.

—Really? Wow. Where?

—The little bits, she said. —They're marshmallows.

—The pink hearts?

—Yes, yes. The pink hearts.

—Then I won't eat the pink hearts. Can we get it if I don't eat the pink hearts? I'll only eat the yellow moons, okay?

—Stop bothering me. The yellow moons are also marshmallows.

—The yellow moons are also marshmallows? Are you sure? What about the green clovers? I think you're wrong about the pink hearts, Mom . . .

She wouldn't budge.

At the moment of man's creation, God had placed within him two inclinations, one good, the other evil. Very little is said of the good inclination, but the evil inclination is notorious—he is the snake in the Garden of Eden, the nakedness of Lot before his daughters, the visitor who encourages Sarah to laugh, he is the man at the back of a crowd of terrified Israelites who calls out, "Let us build a golden calf." It is he who makes Hollywood movies and rock music, Fridaynight television and Nabisco Double-Stuffeds, he who makes the sun shine outside when you should be learning Torah inside, he who turns the leaves beautiful colors to lure you from synagogue on the Day of Atonement. He is an instigator, a trickster, a millenniums-old shit-stirrer, and now, I worried, the evil inclination, like a great white in the murky foul waters of my soul, smelled blood.

I began to steal. I stole Twix. I stole Mars bars. When I heard that the liquid center of Freshen Up chewing gum was made with gelatin, I stole a six-pack from Pathmark and spent the night on the floor of the bathroom, sucking the juice out of all forty-two pieces and throwing away the gum. I still harassed my mother for Franken Berry and Lucky Charms—to suddenly stop would have raised her suspicions—and when my incessant nagging for biblically prohibited breakfast cereals became unbearable, she went to the supermarket without me; I'd wait until she had gone, close my bedroom door, sit cross-legged in front of my open underwear drawer, and by the time she returned home, I'd ruined myself for dinner.

—*Dear God,* I thought to myself, my mouth full of stolen Chuckles and Jelly Bellies, —*what's wrong with me?*

I was sick. I was diseased. I was a criminal. I was a Sodomite, an Amorite, a Hittite, a Sinite, a Givite. I was Cain. I was Esau. I was Lot's wife. I wondered what was taking God so long to punish me, to throw me under a bus with a pocketful of Slim Jims, to give me a heart attack mid–Moon Pie, and when I thought that He was—when I felt a stabbing pain in my chest (heart attack) or a sharp pang in my head (brain aneurysm)—I ran to the bathroom and forced my fingers down my throat, trying to regurgitate the sins I had already swallowed, heaving and retching and hoping that God this evening was feeling All-Forgiving, or at least Partially Forgiving, or maybe just Somewhat Exculpatory. Afterward I went back to my bedroom, beat myself in the stomach with my fists, and rocked back and forth on the edge of the bed, holding a bag of Cheez Doodles I desperately, desperately did not want to eat.

7.

*T*he summer before fifth grade, my parents decided to transfer me from the ultra-Orthodox Yeshiva of Spring Valley to the ordinarily Orthodox Torah Academy, just a short walk from our home. As religious an institution as the Yeshiva of Spring Valley had been, it had, of late, along with the rest of the community, been spiraling steadily upward: gray hats became black hats, carefully trimmed goatees became carefully untrimmed beards, and secular studies such as math and science—always an afterthought—were now the thought that came after the afterthought, if they came at all.

I was nervous. My rabbis at Yeshiva of Spring Valley told me I was going to be the next great rabbi of the Jewish people. They told me I was going to be a leader of my generation. I felt like Abraham, heading off into a strange land full of temptation and sin.

—You're like Abraham, Rabbi Goldfinger said to me when he heard I was leaving, —heading off into a strange land full of temptation and sin.

And what a strange land it was. Instead of the long black

coats my previous rabbis had worn, my new rabbis wore ordinary black suits. Instead of black fedoras, some of them wore gray fedoras. Some of them didn't wear fedoras at all. One of them didn't even have a beard. And yet it was the same religion, the same Torah, the same laws and customs. God was going to smite them all.

—*Dead,* I thought to myself. —*They're all dead.*

The boys wore tiny, non-regulation brightly colored knit yarmulkes instead of enormous black velvet yarmulkes, and instead of letting their *tzitzis* hang out of the side of their pants as God had commanded us, they tucked them in. Some of them had mousse in their hair.

And there were girls.

Short girls, tall girls, blond girls, brunette girls; Deenas and Lisas and Fayes, oh, my. Girls with bows in their hair, girls who smelled like flowers and soap, girls with skirts that danced when they ran and that went swish-swish-swish as they walked down the halls, that crept up their hips as they climbed up the stairs.

All during math class (math class!), tiny, fur-covered creatures scurried around my insides, which was when, under the four watchful horn-rimmed eyes of Rabbi Lehnsherr, boys and girls had class together. Half the boys went into the girls' classroom, and half the girls came into the boys' classroom, and when they did, the room smelled like a meadow, like a thousand meadows, like a thousand meadows covered in a fine, soothing mist of Aqua Net hair spray, and I inhaled deeply as they walked by, the heels of their shiny black shoes making delicate music, clickety-clackety-click, on the hard tile floors.

—Are these graphs in phase? Rabbi Lehnsherr asked one day, pointing to the blackboard.

—In Faye's what? asked Ari.

Everybody laughed.

I thought I was going to puke.

I sat with my head down, as the rabbis from my old yeshiva had advised me, trying to think about Torah, even as the little creatures inside me rolled around on their furry backs and kicked at the air with their tiny, clawed feet.

—*Goners,* I thought. —*Every last one of them.*

By the end of the first week, I wondered if maybe my old rabbis had been right, if maybe I was the next great leader of the Jewish people. Certainly, they would have been proud of me; a stranger in a strange land I may have been, but thus far I was resisting the prurient temptation that King David himself—and Lot and Amnon and Ahab and Zimri and Samson and Lemach—had been unable to resist. And then, one Sunday afternoon, I was playing in the woods behind my house when I discovered a pile of pornographic magazines behind a large boulder at the side of Carlton Road. I picked up a nearby stick and nudged one, gasping as it fell open to a picture of a naked Chinese lady lying on her back. Her legs were spread wide apart. Her finger was inside her vagina. This was what it said below the picture:

Bang my honeypot.

The Sages tell us that the Torah tells us that every day,

God tests us. Sometimes the test is a slice of non-kosher pizza. Sometimes the test is evil gossip. And sometimes the test is a magazine called *Shaved Orientals*.

I dropped the stick and ran.

Deena Seigman snorted when she laughed. Her nose was a little too big, and her eyes a little too close together, but they were beautiful eyes, and it was a beautiful nose, and as she sat in front of me during the too, too brief math class, I stared longingly into her frizzy brown hair and hoped I could die and come back to this life, if only for a moment, as the shiny red hair clip on the top of her head. Often I pretended to be tired, laying my head down on my desk and stretching out my arm so that when she leaned back in her chair, her hair would brush against the back of my hand, and I would close my eyes and press that feeling into my mind, a dried sinful flower, its beauty frozen for eternity. Then she would tut, pull her hair forward over her shoulder, and lean forward.

—Auslander, Rabbi Lehnsherr would call. —Sit up.

Rabbi Lehnsherr stood at the front of the class, pointing out the different objects he had drawn on the blackboard: trapezoid, rhombus, ellipse. All I could think about was one object: honeypots.

My parents worked until late in the afternoon, and because of the shorter hours at my new yeshiva, I now had more time at home alone than I ever had before. I tried to busy myself, tried to keep my mind off Deena and honeypots and the Stone of Pornography waiting for me at the far end of the woods. Some days I raked leaves. Some days I did some laundry. One day, at the bottom of the hamper I found a pair of my mother's tan panty hose.

And the Lord tested Abraham.

I laid them on the floor and stuffed them with the rest of the dirty laundry—socks, T-shirts, hand towels. When the legs were full, I took some duct tape from my father's garage, taped the waistband shut and carried her into my bedroom. She was heavy. One leg was fatter than the other, and the skinny leg was longer than the fatter one. I dropped them onto my bed, wiped my brow, and sat down beside them.

I crossed them.

I uncrossed them.

In the coat closet at the top of the stairs, I found a pair of my mother's high-heeled shoes, hurried down to my bed-room, and put them on her. It. Them. The feet. As I was slowly spreading the legs apart, trying to reproduce the pose of the shaved Oriental I had seen in the magazine, I heard my father's car in the driveway. I flew into a desperate panic, frantically trying to tear the duct tape off the panty hose. I thought about just burying her—it—at the bottom of my closet, but I couldn't handle the humiliation if she were ever discovered. The more I struggled with the tape, the tighter it seemed to hold; my only chance would be to chew my way through it. With the waistband of my mother's stuffed pantyhose between my teeth, I heard my father's car door slam shut and, a few moments later, the front door open.

—Shalom, he called flatly.

I kept chewing. The combination of my biting and saliva was loosening the tape, and I was finally able to yank it off.

—Shalom! he called again.

—Yeah, I called back, pulling laundry out of the panty hose as fast as I could.

He started down the stairs. I had the legs upside down, shaking them, swinging them wildly up and down, shoving my hands deep into the legs and grabbing whatever I could. My father appeared in the doorway just as I was pulling the last few socks from the toes of the left leg.

The floor was littered with dirty pillowcases, shirts, and socks. My bed was covered with soiled linens, damp bath towels, and assorted underwear. And there I sat, in the middle of it all, my arm stuck up the leg of my mother's panty hose.

—What the hell are you doing? he asked.

—Laundry?

—You're doing laundry?

—I'm not?

His eyes narrowed and he looked around the room, searching for clues. He spotted the roll of duct tape on my desk and picked it up.

—What did I tell you about going in my garage? he said.

The garage was strictly off-limits, as was the shed, the closet under the stairs, the attic, and the master bedroom.

—I catch you in there again, he said, —and I'll break your goddamn hands.

He left and went back upstairs. I gathered the laundry

together and put it back in the hamper. My mother came home a few minutes later, and asked if I would help her cook before tackling my homework. Rosh Hashana, the Jewish New Year, was just a couple of weeks away, and my mother liked to get the cooking done early. I changed out of my school clothes and met her in the kitchen, grateful for even the short-lived distraction from honeypots another chore could provide. Unfortunately, to symbolize the hope for a sweet new year, many Rosh Hashana foods include honey.

—Hand me that pot, honey, said my mother. —Where's the pot of honey? —How much honey did you put in that pot? —Must you bang the pots?

—I'll be right back, I said.

I went downstairs, crept out the back door, and hurried back through the woods to the Stone of Pornography. The magazines I had found a few days earlier were gone, but behind another nearby boulder, I discovered a pile of new magazines. It was the hand of God and I knew it—if He could speak to Moses from a bush that was on fire but was never consumed, was it too much to imagine that He could speak to me from a pile of pornography that was never exhausted? I took them home, hid them underneath my bed, and when I had finished helping my mother prepare for the Day of Judgment, I sat on the floor of my bedroom and studied them like Torah. One of the magazines was named *Juggs*, one was named *Forum*, and one was named *Oui*, which I pronounced ow-ee, which sounded like Avi, which was short for Avraham, which was the Hebrew name for Abraham, our forefather. Rabbi Napier had told us that God tested Abraham by commanding him to sacrifice his son Isaac on the top of Mount Moriah. Abraham took Isaac to the mountaintop and laid him down on his back upon a stone, the trees behind them, the skies above, and in Abraham's hand, a sharpened knife he drew high above his son's neck.

—Whoa, whoa, whoa, said God. —Slow down, Killer.

—Such was the greatness of Abraham, Rabbi Napier had said.

Pornography was my Isaac, and I failed.

A few days later, I came home once again to an empty house. I took the magazines outside to the concrete walkway behind the house, whereupon I laid them down there, anointed them with lighter fluid, and set them on fire, a hardcore XXX sin offering to the Lord.

—I am going to destroy the wicked city of Sodom, God said to Abraham.

—What if I find fifty righteous people there? asked Abraham. —Will you destroy the righteous along with the wicked?

God said He wouldn't.

—What if I find forty-five? asked Abraham.

—Yeah, I guess . . .

—Forty?

—Sure, forty. Okay.

I hoped God was still open to a little haggling. I covered my face with my hands, squeezed my eyes shut, and rocked back and forth in front of the fire.

—Please, I begged God. —Test me again. Double or nothing.

Deena didn't pay me much attention. I became painfully aware of my clothing.

All the cool kids wore sweaters with little animals on the chest—alligators, tigers, a tiny man on a tiny horse, preparing to bash its tiny horse face in with his tiny raised mallet. They all wore deck shoes, though few had ever been on a boat, and someone had decided, without telling me, that velour shirts were "in." I cursed my non-velour shirts, hated my non-animal sweaters, loathed my non-boat shoes. Even my yarmulke was wrong. All the cool kids had small, colorful crocheted yarmulkes, half the size of mine, each with elaborate designs—steps and swirls and New York Yankees logos and their names woven right into the border. And there I was with an enormous black velvet yarmulke—no steps, no swirls, no logos. I might as well have been wearing a fucking *tallis*.

I came home one afternoon, went into my father's garage and tightened my yarmulke in the bench-top vise. I took the awl from the pegboard and, holding the edge of the yarmulke up, punched half a dozen holes in the yarmulke's lining. I stuck my fingers in the holes and pulled, tearing the lining this way and that until it was shredded and the edge trim had begun to unravel.

—What the hell happened to it? my mother asked me when she came home.

—It flew off, I said. —I was riding my bike.

—Into what, she asked, —a lawn mower?

—We better get going, I said.

We drove to the Judaica store, where, at the bottom of a bin full of yarmulkes with generic geometric patterns, a few with Jewish stars on them, and one that read *Shabbos, Shabbos, Shabbos* around the edge (—No, I said to my mother before she could recommend it) I found it—a bright blue knit yarmulke with my name on it. My name means "peace," so it shows up a lot in Judaica stores: on challah covers, wall signs, tallis bags, menorahs, seder plates, umbrellas, keychains. Still, I took this as another sign from God: —*Passeth My test,* saith the Lord, —*and Deena shall surely be thine.*

—*Deal,* I said to God. —I burned the porn, you know.

We got home and I locked myself in the bathroom, modeling my new yarmulke in the full-length mirror that hung on the back of the door: turning left, turning right, hands in my front pockets, hands in my back pockets, arms folded across my chest. I tried different positions: I tried wearing it at the front of my head, just above the hairline, like the light on a miner's helmet; I tried wearing it on the back of my head; I slid it back on top and nudged sort of casually off to the side. Damn, they *all* looked good. It was a hell of a yarmulke. Deena wouldn't know what hit her.

—*Honeypot,* I thought.

—I wonder, said the evil inclination, —if you left any magazines under the dresser?

I got down on my hands and knees and looked under my dresser. All gone.

—Maybe your brother's got some? he said.

I checked under my brother's dresser, but there was nothing there, either. I checked under his bed, and I checked inside his closet, and I checked inside his desk. Nothing.

—Behind his books, said the evil inclination.

I stood on my brother's bed, reached behind his books, and pulled out a glossy color magazine. It was called *Puritan,* and my sinful heart began to race.

Where did my brother get a dirty magazine?

Did he know about the Stone of Pornography?

Most important, what was "cum," and why did the woman on the cover want me to shoot it all over her face?

That night, long after my brother and I had fallen asleep, my father kicked open the door to our bedroom. We both jumped. He flicked on the lights, we shielded our eyes, and he demanded to know which one of us had been in his garage. In his angry hand he held the awl I had used earlier that day to mangle my yarmulke, and he pointed it at us as he spoke.

—I catch either of you in my garage again, he growled, —and I'll break your goddamn arms.

He turned, slammed the door, and stomped back upstairs. My brother punched me in the arm, and I tried to punch him back but missed, and he punched me again, and then we both crept quietly out of our bedroom and we tiptoed in our underwear to the foot of the stairs, where we danced around in silent circles, arms extended overhead, our middle fingers pointing up at our father, until it grew too cold and we hurried back to bed, climbed under the covers, and tried to sleep.

The following day, I came home again to an empty house. I carried my brother's magazines outside, drenched them with lighter fluid, and set them on fire.

—What if I find thirty? Abraham asked God. —If you won't destroy Sodom for forty righteous people, will you destroy it for thirty?

God sighed.

—No, He said. —Thirty sounds about . . .

—Twenty?

—Fine, twenty.

—Make it fifteen, said Abraham.

I covered my face with my hands, squeezed my eyes shut and rocked back and forth in front of the fire.

—Please, I begged God. —Best two out of three.

—Deena wants to invite you to her house this *Shabbos,* said Ari.

Ari and Deena were best friends. Ari had an enormous head—he reminded me of a political cartoon come to life— and a mouth full of metal braces and rubber bands. Deena had crocheted him three yarmulkes, but they were only friend yarmulkes, not boyfriend yarmulkes. Ari was also friends with Dov and Eli and another Ari, and Deena was friendly with Lisa and Nava and another Deena, and every Saturday after-

noon Ari and Dov and Eli and the other Ari and Lisa and
Nava and Drorit and the other Deena all walked to Deena's
house to talk about their hair and ridicule their classmates'
clothing. Partly because I felt bad for Ari—one of his nick-
names was Head—but mostly because I knew he was Deena's
friend, I had made a determined effort to become his friend,
and I spent those first few weeks at my new yeshiva laughing
at his stupid jokes and feeding him Stella D'Oro Swiss fudge
cookies. Ari had a thing for Stella D'Oro Swiss fudge cookies.
His other nickname was Stella.

—So you wanna come? Stella asked.

Deena's house was well over an hour's walk away from
mine.

—Sure, I said casually, reaching up to adjust my new yarmulke. —She's really nice.

—I know, said Head. His voice dropped to a whisper and
he leaned toward me. —*I'm trying to set her up with Dov!*

Ari smiled broadly, his freak bobble-head nodding with
excitement. I nodded with him, even as my soul blackened.
Swiss fudge dripped like blood from his braces, and stray
cookie crumbs clung desperately to the edge of his gaping
maw as God reached for my chest, tore through my flesh,
and pulled out my still-beating heart.

I thought about it all day long, and I thought about it some
more as I walked home from school that day. It didn't make
any sense. I could understand if God wanted to punish me

last week, or the week before. Back then our house had been riddled with pornography; our home had been a den of iniquity, a nest of impurity, a split-level ranch of evil. The Sages said spilling semen was a crime worse than murder, so I could understand God punishing me for bringing a gun, so to speak, into the house. But I had burned it all last night, every last page of it—why would He punish me now, after I had purified my soul and cleansed my house? *Unless,* I realized, coming to a dead stop at the foot of Pine Road, *unless there was still more porno in the house.*

I ran.

It was Friday afternoon, and I had a good couple of hours before anyone else got home. I hurriedly checked every inch of our bedroom—the top of the closet and the bottom of the closet, above the dresser and below the dresser, under the beds, under the mattresses, under the desks, under the nightstands. I checked in the bathroom— in the medicine chest, behind the medicine chest, at the bottom of the hamper, underneath the hamper. At last I checked in the laundry room.

There was a magazine called *Swank* under the washing machine that I'd hidden earlier and forgotten about, and under the dryer, a copy of *Juggs*—also one of mine. But I found a *Leg Show* behind the boiler and a *Nugget* behind the sewing table, neither of which I'd ever seen before. On the cover of *Nugget,* a man was urinating on a naked lady. She seemed to be enjoying it, which made me feel slightly better about myself, but significantly worse about my family. Whose magazines were these? My brother's? My father's? Who, precisely, wanted to pee on whom?

I carried the magazines outside, doused them with lighter fluid and set them on fire. I didn't have time to pray. —Best of five, I shouted up to God, as I hurried back inside. —Best of five!

I ran to the garage, took a screwdriver from the pegboard, and headed upstairs. There was no denying that, thanks to *Leg Show* and *Nugget* and a fair degree of personal charm, Dov had a pretty good head start on me in terms of winning Deena's hand. But the race wasn't over yet, I thought as I raced up the stairs. If I had to use mousse, so help me God, I'd use mousse.

The door to my parents' bedroom was locked, as it usually was. I went out back to the deck, pushed a chair over to their bathroom window, forced the blade of the screwdriver under the frame of the screen and popped it out. I moved quickly, sliding open the window, slithering on my stomach through the frame to the bathroom sink below, flipping myself over and landing on the bathroom floor. I replaced the screen, closed the window, and opened the cabinet above the sink. There was volumizing mousse, mousse with extra hold, mousse with extra body, and mousse with both extra body and extra hold. A "dollop"? How much was a dollop? I grabbed the can with extra everything, opened the bathroom door, and was heading for their bedroom door when I noticed something beneath the corner of my father's mattress.

—Go on, said the evil inclination. —You've got time.

The magazine was called *Penthouse*. There was another magazine in his bedside table, mostly of dirty stories, that was called *Variations*. I wondered how many tests my father had failed. Which test was he up to—the tenth? The twentieth? How was God punishing him? With me? With a sinner for a son? Would I have a sinner for a son, too? Beneath the shirts in his dresser I found a book called *101 Sexual Positions,* and briefly pictured Deena in all 101 of them before opening the door of their bedroom and heading out.

—What about her? asked the evil inclination.

I stopped and turned around. He was talking about my mother.

—Don't be ridiculous, I answered.

My mother came from a very distinguished family of rabbis. Her brother was a rabbi, and her other brother was a rabbi. Her uncles were rabbis, and her grandfather was a rabbi. Two of her nephews were rabbis, and two of her nieces married rabbis. In the hallway, on the wall across from their bedroom, hung fading black-and-white photographs of her ancestors in their long black coats and big black hats.

—Have it your way, said the evil inclination. —But Deena's pretty cute. I'm just saying. Personally, if it were me, I wouldn't risk it.

I checked in my mother's nightstand. I checked under her mattress. I checked in her closet and I checked in her makeup table. Underneath her bed, I found a small pink box. Inside the pink box was a white stick with a dial on the bottom. When I turned the dial, the stick began to buzz and vibrate. There were also a few different flesh-colored plastic sleeves that fit over the vibrator, one with small nubs all over it, one with ridges up and down it, and one shaped like a penis, only much bigger. Curious to see what it would feel like to have such a penis, I lay down on my mother's bed, pulled down my pants, and put my own smaller penis inside the giant plastic one.

It was very smooth.

After a few minutes, I understood all that I had seen in those magazines. I knew what looked like pain but wasn't, and I knew what the Torah meant when it said a man knew a woman, and I knew it didn't have anything to do with knowing. I looked down at the seed I had spilled on my belly and wanted to cry; if it had taken me four months to figure out how to get it out, it was going to take me twice that long to figure out how to put it back in, and I didn't have that kind of time. From their perch on the wall outside the bedroom doorway, my fading black-and-white ancestors frowned down at me, disgusted and disappointed.

—*Is this,* they grumbled, —*what we died in the Holocaust for?*

I cleaned myself off and carried it all outside—the *Penthouse,* the *Variations,* my father's book of sexual positions, and my mother's box of penises, and lit them all on fire.

Eventually, Abraham had haggled God down to ten—if he could find ten righteous people in Sodom, God would agree to spare the city. Abraham looked and looked, but he couldn't find any.

I was having the same kind of luck.

I covered my face with my hands and rocked back and forth in front of the fire.

—Best of seven, I begged the Lord. —Please, please, please, best of seven.

That night, long after we had fallen asleep, my father kicked open the door to our bedroom and we both jumped. He stood there in his underwear, breathing heavily through his nose, demanding to know which one of us had been in his bedroom.

—Which one of you *ganif*s went in there? he growled through clenched teeth. A *ganif* is a thief. He had been drinking. He steadied himself on the doorknob.

—I don't know what you're talking about, said my brother.

—Up, said my father.

Neither of us moved.

—Why? my brother asked.

My father slammed his fist into the door, cracking the wood. My hands began to shake.

—*Up!*

We climbed out of bed and huddled together as my father marched us out of the bedroom into the den next door, where he made us stand side by side in our underwear, shivering in the cold night air.

—You'll stand there all night, he said.

We stood there for a very long time. I thought of Deena, asleep somewhere in her warm flowery bed, and of Dov, a smile on his face, asleep somewhere in his own. If God was ever going to destroy this Sodom of ours, I hoped he would do it now. I heard the door to my parents' bedroom creak open and the sound of my mother's soft footsteps heading down the hall. They came to a stop at the top of the stairs.

—That's enough, she called down.

—Go to bed, said my father.

She stood there a moment longer.

—Go to bed! he shouted, and she did. After what seemed like hours, he stood up, walked toward us, and leaned over so that his face was even with ours.

—I catch you in my room again, he said, —and I'll break your goddamn arms.

My brother looked at me and rolled his eyes, and my father smacked him across the face with the back of his hand.

My brother covered his face with his hands. I could tell that he was trying not to cry, but his eyes filled with tears anyway. So did mine, and when I looked up at my father, his eyes were full of tears, too. He turned and stomped upstairs.

What was God thinking? What was He doing to us? Tearing us apart, pitting us against one another like this, father against son, brother against brother? When I heard my father's heavy footsteps move down the hall and the door to his bedroom finally lock shut behind him, I tiptoed to the foot of the stairs, where I held both my middle fingers up— one for my father, one for God—and started to dance in a circle, hoping my brother would join me, but he just stamped once on the floor, threw a punch at the air, and went back to bed. Soon it became cold, but I could hear my brother sobbing, so I waited for a while before going in.

—*Well?* I thought to God as I climbed beneath the covers. —*Are You happy now? Are You happy now, You big stupid jerk?*

He wasn't.

The walk to Deena's house was a difficult one. It was an unusually hot day, and I was sleepy after last night's interrogation. I walked up Carlton Road, past the synagogue, through the backyard of the Gartenbergs' house, past the other synagogue, all the way to Briarcliff Lane. By the time I got there, the super-hold anti-frizz styling mousse was dripping down my forehead and staining the collar of my shirt, which I had washed and ironed for just this occasion. I tried to wipe the mousse off my shirt with the back of my tie, but it was no use. All-day hold, my ass.

Ari answered the door. Eli and the other Ari and Lisa and Nava and Drorit and the other Deena were all in the den. Dov and Deena were out for a walk.

—Oh, I said.

When they came back, Dov was smiling. He had asked Deena to be his girlfriend, and Deena had accepted. The other Ari high-fived Dov, and Drorit asked Deena what color yarmulke she was going to make for him.

I stayed a little while longer, before announcing that it was quite a long walk home, and that I had better get going.

As I trudged down Deena's driveway, hands shoved deep in my pockets, the slowly rehardening mousse a superhold helmet of shame upon my head, it occurred to me that maybe it wasn't so much that my father on Earth was like my Father in Heaven, but that my Father in Heaven was like my father on Earth. That maybe if God gave you a test that He thought you could pass, He got really pissed off if you failed—not because you failed, but because He didn't like being wrong. And maybe when God got pissed off, He made his way downstairs to Earth, kicked in the door to your world, and threatened to break your goddamn arms. Or your goddamn heart. Or whatever else He could get His goddamn hands on.

—Shalom! someone called.

I stopped and turned around. It was Deena. She was skipping and running toward me, her skirt dancing, creeping up her hips, and for a moment I thought, —*Maybe* . . .

She came over to my side, and I could feel her warm, soft hair on my face, and feel her even warmer, softer breath on my ear. I thought for a moment that maybe I should turn and kiss her.

—Lisa really likes you! she whispered.

Lisa was Deena's best friend. She had black hair and dark rings around her eyes. Good one, God.

—I like her, too, I said to Deena.

Sinners can't be choosers.

—*Yay!* cheered Deena, and ran back to her house to give Lisa the news.

8.

I am thirty-five years old, and I am disgusting.

Blacks, whites, Asians, midgets. Big tits, small tits, real tits, fake tits. Domination, humiliation, fisting, felching. Heterosexuals, homosexuals, bisexuals, transsexuals.

There is something wrong with me. Maybe it's a disease I picked up. Maybe there is a pill I can swallow. Libiditrol. Depravex. Flaccidia.

I think disgusting things on the way to the office. I think disgusting things while I am in the office. I think disgusting things on the way home from the office. I am adrift in a sea of ass. Ass on the sidewalk in front of me, ass on the subway pressed up against me, beside me in elevators, passing me in hallways. This isn't some Philip Roth sexual-obsession-as-a-reflection-of-man's-fear-of-death disgusting. This is not my physical being yearning for higher illumination. There is no greater existential message within my degeneracy. This is not *Sabbath's Theater*; it is *Shalom's Buddy Booth*. I'm gross. I'm icky. I'm wicked.

There is bondage on the uptown F train, sodomy on the

downtown R. There is an imaginary gang bang on the Forty-second Street crosstown bus. Board meetings become orgies. A nervous interviewee becomes a captive sex slave; a presentation by a female executive becomes a strip show, a lap dance, a blow job beneath the austere oak table (because, in a way, of the austere oak table). I am disgusting.

Here's the punch line:

—What's wrong? asks Orli.

—Nothing.

—Not in the mood?

—Whatever.

Awkwardness.

—Mind if I have a go? she asks.

She finishes quickly.

—You're gifted, I say.

She laughs, rolls off me.

I swing my legs over the side of the bed. The blinds are open and I can see the moon, and the stars, and the dark night sky beyond, where God is sitting on His front porch, laughing at me. Laughing and laughing and laughing. —*All those years of wasting sperm without a woman,* He says to His cronies beside Him, —*and now he can't get off with one!* Abraham laughs and slaps God on the back.

Good one, God.

I shake my head.

—I don't understand, I say. —You'd think I was sexually abused.

—You were theologically abused, says Orli. —That's much worse.

Speaking of his sexual desires, the poet Max Jacob wrote, —*Heaven will pardon me for the pleasures which it knows are involuntary.* A few years later, Heaven killed Max in a German concentration camp.

This is the term we've been using lately: *theological abuse.* It involves adults, known or unknown to the underage victim, telling them a Lunatic runs the world, that He's spying on them, that He's waiting for them to break a rule.

God is here,
God is there,
God is truly
everywhere!
So watch it, kid.

Other choices included "spiritually groped," "religiously fingered," and "touched inappropriately by an angel."

So now we're blaming God, is that it? You can't get off and somehow it's God's fault?

Yes.

9

*R*abbi Blowfeld led us silently through the hallway to the darkened auditorium at the far side of the school. Nobody spoke as we took our seats. On the stage at the front of the room, Israeli flags stood on either side of a large movie screen. On the screen was a joyous little girl who was dead. Her name was Anne Frank. We spent the morning watching terrifying movies and graphic newsreel footage. Some of the girls cried. In one scene, a Nazi soldier was using a bulldozer to lift bodies into a waiting dump truck. As the bucket scooped and lifted, one of the bodies at the top of pile rolled down the side. Her arms seemed to wave as she rolled; her head, like a heavy burden, fell back between her shoulders. She tumbled, fell, landed in a broken heap. Between her legs, a dark nest of pubic hair came into view. I glanced at Eli, and Eli glanced at me, and we quickly looked away. It was the first naked Jewish girl I had ever seen. I was eleven. She was dead. It was Holocaust Remembrance Day.

—The Torah tells us, said Rabbi Blowfeld, —that God

passed over the houses of the Jews the night He brought the tenth and final plague upon the Egyptians.

—Why did He have to "pass over" their houses? asked Rabbi Blowfeld.

—Because, answered Rabbi Blowfeld, —because the Jews were living in Egyptian neighborhoods.

They were assimilating.

—Same thing, he said, turning to look up at Anne Frank, —same thing.

When I got home, the dining room was the living room. The living room was the dining room.

—Well? asked my mother.

She was standing in the corner of the dining room that used to be the living room, one hand on her hip, the other on her chin, one eye closed tightly as she squinted at the new layout with the other.

Every room in our house contained at least one magazine basket, and every basket was overflowing with dog-eared decorating magazines. *Better Homes and Gardens, Traditional Home, Dream Houses.* There was a magazine named *Kitchens.* There was a magazine named *Baths.* There was a magazine named *Kitchens and Baths.*

—If you didn't spend all my money on magazines, my father would say to my mother, —maybe we could afford to do something around here.

—What do you think? she asked me.

She shifted, and in one practiced, fluid movement, the hand on her hip went to her chin, the hand on her chin went to her hip, she closed the eye she had been squinting with and squinted with the one she'd had closed. *Was this,* she seemed to be trying to figure out, *a better home and garden, or was it a worse home and garden?* Usually she decided it was just the same old goddamned home and garden, and, enlisting my help, would move everything back where it came from.

—I like it, I said.

She squinted a moment longer before giving up.

—Your father will hate it, she said. —Help me move it back before he gets home.

We moved the couch against the wall and were in the middle of dragging the dining table back to the dining room when the telephone rang and my mother went to the kitchen to answer it.

—*Hello? Oh, hi, Leslie.*

I finished pushing the dining table back, and turned to the living room window just in time to see Lince Rivera run by.

—*Yes,* I heard my mother say. *Yes, I'd heard that.*

We lived on a dead-end street named Arrowhead Lane; our house was at the bottom, where the street died. Arrowhead Lane was on the western edge of Monsey—according to the post office it was Suffern—and ours was one of the few roads in the area that wasn't predominantly Jewish: there were two Jewish families—us and the Baums—a Polish family named Petrulo ("no-good Nazis"), two Irish families, the Kilduffs and the Delaneys ("classic Jew-haters"), and one Italian family, the Selernos. And there, at the top of the road, in the yellow split-level ranch with the broken-down Pontiac in the driveway and the sign on the front yard that read "Dead End," was the black family. The Riveras. Lince was eighteen. Her brother Leon was a year older than I, her brother Lionel a year younger.

—*Tut, tut, tut. How is she taking it?*

Lince was a runner, a track star at her public high school, and she ran almost every day. I had never really noticed her before. Now, though, I couldn't take my eyes off her. In her tight running shorts and tighter-still tank top, she seemed to be made of solid stone.

My mother walked back in the room and snapped her fingers to get my attention. I turned around. She pointed to the phone.

—*Mrs. Pleeter's father,* she mouthed.

She drew her index finger across her throat.

—Blessed is the One True Judge, she said in Hebrew into the phone as she shuffled sadly back into the kitchen. —Blessed is the One True Judge.

Lince had made her way around the cul-de-sac and was headed back up the hill; as captivated as I had been by her running toward me, I was even more transfixed by her running away. She had muscles where I didn't even know muscles could be, on her thighs, her shoulders, her back. The women around me didn't have muscles. They had grocery bags, and worries, and burdens, and thin blue veins of exhaustion that snaked up the backs of their thick, pale legs. Their bodies seemed to point to the ground; their breasts, their bottoms, even their backs hunched over, their bodies seemingly eager to begin the inexorable descent to the grave. Lince's parts pointed straight into the air, defiant, alive.

My mother came back into the living room, her face long and drawn as she dialed the phone. She groaned as she sat on the couch.

—Hi, Sally? she said into the phone. —I have some bad news.

When I turned back to the window, Lince was gone.

The next day, I went with my mother to Caldor's department store on Route 59. She went to look for a condolence card for Mrs. Pleeter, and I went and flipped through the book of the movie *Porky's*. She finished before I did, and met me at the book section. She was having a difficult time deciding between "You are in our thoughts in your time of need" and "We are with you in your sorrow."

—Well? she asked.

I didn't answer. I was halfway through the hole-in-the-shower-wall chapter, and the high school girls were just beginning to undress. What a life.

—Enough, she said to me, taking the book from my hands. —It's almost *Shabbos*.

—*What's it like here on Saturdays?* I wondered.

I didn't like Sabbath. I didn't like the meals, I didn't like the rules, I didn't like the clothes. I didn't like the dress pants and the dress shirts and the blazers, and I didn't like the way ties felt around my neck. I didn't like the way shoes looked on my feet, or the way they slid on the carpet, or the sound they made on the street when I was walking to synagogue. I didn't like walking to synagogue. I didn't like synagogue. I didn't like being separated from the women, and I didn't like being stuck with the men. I didn't like standing there for hours at the mercy of the cantor with the sun shining outside and the birds singing and the whole world enjoying the day, thinking, —*Shut up, shut up, shut up, will you just shut up?*

When we got home, I hid my bicycle in the tall grass of the field behind our house. That night, after Sabbath began, my brother provoked my father, my father slapped my brother, my mother yelled at my father, my sister ran crying to her room, my mother went outside for a walk, and I cleaned off the Sabbath table and put away the chicken. Rabbi Blowfeld told us that every Friday night, God sends two angels down to Earth, where they visit every Jewish household and peek in the windows to see what kind of Sabbath they are having. If the family is singing Sabbath songs and everyone is happy and honoring the Sabbath, the angels look at one another and smile and say, —So shall it be next Sabbath. And if they look in the window and see the family fighting, not singing Sabbath songs, and not honoring the Sabbath?

—So shall it be next Sabbath, they say.

Saturday, after morning services, we ate lunch while my mother told us who was sick.

—Sally Fried's mother-in-law, she said. —Doesn't look good.

—I saw Toby. They're doing whatever they can—takes a bit of challah. —They can't do anything.

—Helen looked good.

Wait for it.

—For someone with cancer, I mean.

—*Screw this,* I thought. —*I'm going to Caldor's.*

After dessert and the latest on Mr. Rosner's enlarged prostate, I went to my bedroom, put on my sneakers, and went quietly out the back door. I found my bicycle in the field, pushed it through the grass to Spook Rock Road, hopped on, and rode up Spook Rock to Airmont Road. I turned right and rode two miles to Route 59, where I turned left again and rode until I came to Caldor's. I leaned my bicycle against the side of the building and was about to go inside when the man before me stepped on the black rubber mat, causing the door to open.

I stood there for some time.

I knew it would be a violation of the Sabbath if I stepped on the mat and caused the door to be opened, but would it be a violation if someone else stepped on the mat and I followed them in?

—Excuse me, a man said as he roughly pushed past me.

Obviously, riding a bicycle was also prohibited on Sabbath, but it didn't involve electricity, and how else was I supposed to get there?

—Bad place to stand, kid, said another customer walking by.

There was a steel door to the side of the electric door, but it was marked Emergency, and what if I went through and set off some sort of alarm? On top of that, Caldor's was air-conditioned—even if I went in through the emergency door, wouldn't opening the door allow warm air in and trigger the air-conditioning? What if something I was wearing set off the security alarm? Were unintentional violations of the Sabbath punished less severely than intentional ones? What if God already decided to punish me for riding my bicycle? Would He kill me? Would He kill my family? Was He killing them right now? Hadn't I just heard a fire engine go by? Was it going to my house? Were they all dead?

I jumped back on my bicycle and rode home as fast as I could. I dumped the bike in the field and hurried through the woods, relieved momentarily at the lack of fire and rescue surrounding our house until I realized it might just be a setup and they were all dead inside—a murder, a gas leak, you never know. I crept quietly through the back door, took off my sneakers, and went upstairs, silently promising God I would never violate the Sabbath again.

—*Khuchuuuungnk,* said my father.

He was asleep on the living room floor, snoring loudly. My mother was tucked up on the couch reading *House Beautiful.*

—Where have you been? she asked.

—At Dov's house.

She flipped through the pages of the magazine and shook her head sadly.

—It's nice to dream, she sighed.

—*Wheeeze-gchuk*, said my father.

I went into the kitchen, made a cup of tea, sat down beside my mother, and looked outside. Lince ran by.

—Wow, I whispered.

—No kidding, said my mother. —You know how much a sunroom like that costs?

—I'm going for a walk, I said.

Lince was cooling down in her driveway when I walked by. She had one hand on her car, the other hand grabbing her instep, as she stretched those thoroughbred legs and rolled that long, powerful neck. I walked by, trying not to look like I was trying to look, and turned left on Carlton Road, which brought me around the side of their house. From there I could look across the front lawn and see her through the trees. The front door swung open and I jumped. It was Leon, Lince's brother, and some of his friends.

Leon was one year older than me. We used to play together—Leon, his younger brother, Lionel, and I—in the woods behind our homes. Afterward, we would sit in Leon's room and read comic books.

—You want one? Lionel asked one Friday afternoon, holding up a Twinkie.

—Shellum can't eat that, you idiot, said Leon.

—Why not?

—He's kosher.

—So?

Leon shook his head.

—Shellum, Leon asked me, —is Twinkies kosher?

I shook my head.

—It's okay, I said.

—See? said Leon, grabbing my Twinkie from Lionel's hand. —Stupid.

—Damn, said Lionel. —You can't *never* eat a Twinkie?

I shrugged.

—They might be kosher someday, I said. —After the messiah comes.

—What's the messiah? asked Lionel.

—The end of the world, I said.

Leon took a bite of my Twinkie.

—Damn, he said to himself. Then he looked to Lionel. —I don't think we have no kosher, do we?

—I don't know, said Lionel. He looked to me. —Do we?

I shrugged.

—Do you have apples?

—Yeah, we have apples, said Leon.

—Apples are kosher, I said.

—Do you want one? asked Leon.

—Nah.

Leon got up and brought me an apple.

—Thanks, I said.

—Can I try on your beanie? asked Lionel.

Leon tutted at him and shook his head.

—Sure, I said.

Lionel tried it on, but he had an afro and it just sort of sat on top of his head without settling in. Leon had tight cornrows, so it fit better on him. He stood up slowly and tried to walk around, stepping lightly as if he were trying to balance a book on his head.

—Damn, he said.

That was a few years ago; lately, ever since Leon began junior high, we hadn't spoken much. Our friendship seemed to wither as new friends entered our world: friends of his who wondered why he was talking to me, friends of mine who wondered why I was talking to him. Hellos became waves. Waves become nods.

As Leon headed down the walkway to his driveway that Saturday afternoon, he spotted me walking by. I half waved. He half nodded. One of his friends smiled. The other friend laughed and punched Leon in the arm. All three went into the garage.

I walked to Pine Road, turned around, stopped off at the Stone of Pornography (nothing), and headed back home.

—*Khcuhngzk,* said my father when I returned home.

I didn't like Sabbath.

Saturday nights weren't much better. —*Blessed are You,* we prayed at the conclusion of the Sabbath, —*who separates between the holy and the profane.* My brother was living at his high school dormitory and came home only for the weekend. Saturday nights, when he left, the freedom of the forthcoming week beckoned and he was more contentious with my father than usual. If God had really wanted to impress me, He'd have separated my brother from my father. That night, they nearly came to blows. They stood nose to nose in the hallway outside the kitchen.

—Oh, really? said my brother.

—Oh, really, said my father.

—Really really?

—Really really.

My mother's ineffectual ancestors stared down from their photographs. *Tut tut,* they said. Before the night was over, my father had thrown my brother's brand-new karate uniform in the woodstove and set it on fire.

—The Sabbath, Rabbi Blowfeld said the following Monday morning, —is like a bride. —Like a Gift, he said. —Like a covenant.

Rabbi Blowfeld twisted his beard and looked thoughtfully at the floor for a moment before looking back at the class.

—What else, he asked us, —is Sabbath like?

Like a punishment? Like a curse? Like a sick joke?

—Like a delicate flower? I offered.

Rabbi Blowfeld twisted his beard and looked thoughtfully at the floor for a moment before looking back up.

—Yes, he said. —Like a delicate flower.

Schmuck.

Then he told us that the Sages said that observing the Sabbath was like observing all 613 commandments in the Torah, but that violating the Sabbath was like violating all 613 commandments.

Stupid Sages. Let's see them stay locked in a house with my family for twenty-four hours.

Some gift.

Wednesday we went to the mall.

The Nanuet Mall—with its four-theater movieplex, two electronics stores, three rock-and-roll music stores, and sprawling non-kosher food court—was a two-story brick-faced self-contained city of Sodom. Mothers went to Bamberger's and bought immodest dresses, fathers went to Sears and bought tools unrelated to Torah study. Older kids stood outside the main entrance, smoking cigarettes and spitting on the floor.

—Dude, one would say.

—Dude, another would answer.

—Fuck this, the first would say.

—Fuck that, his friend would answer.

I wanted to live there.

Inside, the younger kids would try to sneak into Spencer Gifts, where they sold whoopee cushions, posters of girls sitting on sports cars wearing tight jeans and open shirts, and pens that showed girls in bikinis, which fell off when you turned the pen upside down.

People from all over Rockland County came to the Nanuet Mall. The white kids wore T-shirts that read "Ozzy" and "Deep Purple," and they gathered at the video arcade, where they got into fights. —Cool it, the security guard would say. The black kids rode BMX bikes to the mall and gathered in the parking lot, where they played loud music on their enormous portable stereos. —Turn it down, the security guard would say. The white kids called the stereos "nigger boxes." The black kids called the white kids "honkies." Both of them laughed when the Chassidim walked by.

—*What's it like here on Saturday?* I wondered.

My mother went off to Bamberger's, and we agreed to meet at Waldenbooks in an hour. I snuck into Spencer's and tried out the whoopee cushion, then went to the back and looked at the posters of girls wearing T-shirts while dousing themselves with garden hoses. After that I went to Waldenbooks, where I sat on the floor with a pile of medical books: *Gray's Anatomy*, *The Making of a Surgeon*, *The Time-Life Guide to the Skeletal System*. I had become obsessed with anatomy; if God was going to kill me with a disease, maybe I could figure out how to cure it. *An ounce of preparation*, read the sign in Dr. Zisman's office, *is worth a pound of cure*. I liked those exchange rates.

After a while, my mother tapped me on the shoulder. She was holding a book in her hands. *The Jewish Way in Death and Mourning*.

—For Mrs. Pleeter, she explained. —Cheer her up a bit.

—*What's it like here on Saturday?* I wondered.

—*Chunngkh*, said my father.

It was Sabbath afternoon—bride afternoon, covenant

126

afternoon, gift afternoon—and I was slumped facedown on the kitchen table, staring past an Entenmann's coffee cake box at the yellowing flip clock on the stovetop across the room. It had been reading 1:59 p.m. for what seemed like hours. At last the top half of the 9 began its infuriatingly laggard fall forward, a slow-motion suicide from the top of the tallest building in Clockland, landing, sometime later, facefirst at its final resting place below.

I yawned.

The chair groaned.

The refrigerator moaned.

It was 2:00 p.m.

My father lay flat on his back on the living room floor, snoring loudly. The comic section of the local newspaper was trapped beneath him.

The Wizard of Id gasped; he wasn't going to make it. Beetle Bailey was long dead. Sarge, too.

—Kid, said Dagwood Bumstead, —get . . . help . . .

—*Khcuhngzk,* said my father.

My mother was curled up on the couch with a cup of tea and a copy of *The Jewish Press.*

—Ten Israeli soldiers killed in Lebanon, she read aloud. —Eighteen years old. Babies.

She would rather have been reading *Romantic Homes* or even *Great Kitchens,* but the temptation to move a couch or relocate the buffet might prove too strong; it was forbidden to rearrange the furniture on the Sabbath. It was forbidden to watch TV, it was forbidden to write, it was forbidden to draw, it was forbidden to color. It was forbidden to play with trains because they used electricity. It was forbidden to play with Legos because it was considered building. It was forbidden to play with Silly Putty because if you pressed it against a newspaper it would transfer some of the ink to itself, and so it was considered printing. All that you were permitted to do was eat, sleep, and read, but no matter how many books I took out of the library on Friday afternoon, I was finished with them all by Friday night, and by Saturday afternoon I was slumped over the kitchen table, reading the side of the Entenmann's doughnut box for the ten thousandth time. The history of Entenmann's, the price per pound of Entenmann's, the ingredients of Entenmann's; I knew more about Entenmann's doughnuts than most of the Entenmanns themselves.

—Another cemetery desecrated in Germany, I heard my mother read. —Six million wasn't enough.

I wondered what it would be like to be an Entenmann. Their house probably smelled like cookies. Saturday mornings, we Entenmanns would all jump out of our beds and race down to the kitchen, where we'd spend all morning dipping doughnuts in huge vats of rich chocolate frosting made of partially hydrogenated vegetable shortening, sugar, flour, malted barley flour, reduced iron, niacin, thiamin mononitrate, riboflavin, folic acid, water, cocoa, nonfat milk, high-fructose corn syrup, dextrose and polysorbate 60.

—*Chazah*, I heard my father say. Pig. —Don't eat all the brownies.

—I had *two,* my brother said. He was at the table in the dining room.

—You had more than two.

My brother must have smiled or made a face. I heard my father get up and stomp into the dining room.

—Something funny? I heard my father ask. Silence for a moment. —Punk.

—Who wants to fill the danishes? Mrs. Entenmann would sing.

—Yayy! we would all cheer, and run to her side.

My father stomped into the kitchen and poured himself a cup of tea.

—What are you doing with those? he asked, looking at the box of Entenmann's doughnuts. —You're *fleishig.*

This meant I had eaten meat recently, and was forbidden from eating anything dairy.

—I'm reading the box.

—Read a different box, he said, pulling it away from me and putting it on top of the refrigerator.

I opened the pantry and took out the Nestlé Quik, which had the history of chocolate on the back. I'd read that one twenty thousand times.

In 1492, Queen Isabella and King Ferdinand . . .

My brother walked by the kitchen with a brownie in his hand. He stopped at the door, took an exaggerated bite, grinned at my father, and walked away. My father, who'd been at the counter cutting an apple, gritted his teeth and made a stabbing motion with the knife. I spotted the angels outside the kitchen window.

—So shall it be next Sabbath, said the one angel.

—So shall it be, said the other.

—Fuck off, I said to them.

The tall one wrote something in his notebook, the short one gave me the finger, and they floated away. I went downstairs and stopped at the front door to watch Lince run by. She circled the cul-de-sac, and headed back up the road.

I went to my bedroom, picked up my wallet (forbidden), took out some money (forbidden), lied to my mother and said I was going to Ari's house (forbidden), and walked out the front door.

—*Fuck this,* I thought, —*I'm going to the mall.*

It was Saturday afternoon and the synagogue was empty; everyone was home, sleeping off their Sabbath lunches and defending the brownies from their children.

—Hello, I whispered into the pay phone. —I need a taxi.

—Speak up, lady, said the dispatcher.

—I said I need a taxi.

—Where you headed?

—The Nanuet Mall.

—Where?

—The Nanuet Mall!

—Where you at? he asked.

—Carlton Road, I whispered.

—Be there in five, ma'am.

It was one thing to use the pay phone on Sabbath—doctors did it all the time. But getting into a car? Going to the mall? That was pretty serious. —*Violating the Sabbath,* I heard Rabbi Blowfeld say, —*was like violating all 613 commandments.* Moses had committed one sin in his whole life, and because of it, God killed him before he could reach the Promised Land. One sin. Sarah laughed—she *chuckled*—and, knowing that one day she would, God had made her barren.

I stood in the vestibule of the synagogue, waiting for my taxi, and wondered how God might punish me for 613 sins. Would He make me barren? Was there a Promised Land I would never reach? Maybe God had already punished me and I didn't know it. Maybe He had killed my family. Maybe He burned down the house while I was walking here. Hadn't I heard sirens earlier? Did killers break in after I had left? Were they in my house right now? Maybe they were tying my family up at this very moment, guns pressed to the side of their heads, and maybe God was waiting to see what I would do—if I left right now, He would make the kidnappers leave. But the moment I got in the cab, He would . . .

I jumped as the cabdriver leaned on his horn. I grabbed my bag, ran outside, dove into the backseat, and slammed the car door shut behind me.

Bam, 613 sins.

—Nanuet Mall? asked the driver.

—*Shh!* I said, holding up my finger to silence him as I listened briefly for gunshots.

Nope.

Nothing.

—Yes, I said. —Nanuet Mall.

I sat in the back of the cab that Sabbath afternoon, not even sure why I was going to the mall—maybe I was hoping to find something, maybe I was hoping to escape something, maybe I just wanted to know that I could go if I wanted to, if I had to—simultaneously violating the Fourth Commandment, the bride, the gift, the covenant and the delicate flower, and I thought again about Moses. One sin, and ka-blammo. I had just racked up 613, and the day wasn't over yet. The same fear that had gripped me outside Caldor's just a few weeks before put its cold, bony hand on my shoulder and drew me close. I slumped down in my seat, stared out the window, and crunched the spiritual numbers:

Okay. No sense denying it—car on Sabbath was a major violation. You weren't just riding in a car—you were assimilating. You were finishing what Hitler had started.

When I was younger I used to walk to synagogue beside my father. My father yelled at cars.

—Slow down! he shouted, stepping into the road and waving his arms over his head. —Kill a Jew, then you'll be happy.

They would swerve wildly to avoid hitting him, and look out the window at us like we were people on TV. Or aliens.

—*Ahnta-Semitin,* he would grumble in Yiddish. Anti-Semites.

I wondered how we must have looked to them, to the people in the cars—out for a Saturday-morning drive along the winding, wooded country roads of Rockland County, thinking about all the lights they were going to switch on and off, of all the television they were going to watch, of all the pig they were going to eat, when suddenly there they were—we were—men in black suits and fedoras; women in long, formal dresses with white lace doilies on their heads; young boys in little blue suits and little white dress shirts and colorful skullcaps; young girls in fancy dresses and shiny shoes—walking along the side of the road; two, sometimes three people abreast, some of the men draped in long white sheets with white strings dangling from the corners, some of them in black-belted bathrobes with furry, circular hats on their closely shaven heads, and one guy, a madman with a silver beard and a furious red face, jumping into the road, waving his arms and shouting about killing the Jews.

The driver gunned the engine as we headed up Carlton Road, tires spinning as we left the synagogue parking lot. He seemed to be in an awful hurry.

Six thirteen in the hole. I could pray three times a day, every day, for the next seven months and still not break even. And who knew when He was going to decide to collect? We drove by a Jewish family—a man and his two children—walking along the side of the road, and I slid further down in my seat and watched them as we drove by.

—*So that's what we look like,* I thought.

I held on to the door handle as the driver made the sharp right onto College Road, tires squealing as he floored it in the direction of Route 59. We were flying—sixty-five in a thirty-five, weaving, honking, passing on the shoulder.

—Late for synagogue? I asked the driver. —Heh-heh. Seriously, no rush.

Maybe he was an angel. Maybe he was Elijah. Had God sent Elijah to teach me a lesson?

—Give him something to think about, God had commanded him.

Elijah grinned madly, dragging his finger across his throat. God shrugged.

—See how it goes, He had said.

Elijah came up fast behind an old woman driving a dull silver hatchback, brown smoke burping from her rusty exhaust. He leaned on the horn and flashed his brights before stomping on the gas and crossing into oncoming traffic to pass her. The old lady frowned at us. Elijah honked and gave her the finger.

Probably not Elijah, then.

We swerved back into our lane just moments before colliding head-on with a blue pickup. I wondered how many Sabbaths my driver had violated, and why God hadn't killed him yet, and if he'd violate Sabbath again next weekend and if I would, too, when I suddenly remembered Rabbi Blowfeld saying the Sages saying that not only is violating the Sabbath like violating all 613 commandments, but that observing the Sabbath is like observing all 613 command-ments, and then it hit me: If I violated Sabbath this weekend but observed it next weekend, trangressionally speaking, wouldn't I pretty much break even?

I smiled. I sure as hell would.

I giggled.

That wasn't just a loophole—it was a license to violate. One "observe" weekend after every "violate" weekend and I'm spiritually debt-free.

Sages? Idiots!

We were approaching Route 59, the four-lane highway that led to Nanuet, when the driver floored it and I was thrown backward against the seat. He wasn't going for the light, was he? It was already yellow . . .

I could observe all January, and violate all February! Observe winter, violate summer! *Shalom's Sage-Certified All-Violate Summer Sin-a-Thon Spectacular!*

Red now, the light. Cars creeping into the intersection. A bus . . .

—Light! I called out.

Hell, I might even start a little "commandment savings account"—string a few "observe" weekends together in a row, build up a little commandment nest egg. A rainy holy day fund.

Faster now. Cars honking. The bus . . .

—Light! I called out again. —LIGHT!

I was going to die. Shit, he *was* Elijah. I closed my eyes and prayed to . . .

Death. Of course! Dying was the monkey wrench in my whole visionary plan: if I died after an "observe" weekend, sure, I'm paid in full, I'm sitting pretty. But if I died after a "violate" weekend—plans to "observe" next Sabbath or not—I died with 613 big ones. Past due.

—But I was going to observe next weekend, I'd plead.

God would shrug and sigh. —I understand, He would say, —but We're trying to run a business here . . .

The car horns faded. I opened my eyes and sat up. We were through—through!—charging up Route 59, speeding again, darting, weaving.

It wasn't a license, after all, it was a trick. At best it was a gamble, at worst it was a dare. A dare from God. —*Step right up, folks, take your chances. Violate this Sabbath, and hope I let you live to observe the next. Who's feeling lucky? How about you, son, you there in the taxicab on* Shabbos *afternoon?*

Take my chances? Was I crazy? With *this* God? With Mr. Vengeance? Mr. Flood the Earth? Mr. Holocaust?

—I'll get out here, I called to the driver.

I thought again about Moses, and I realized what had troubled me about that whole damn story; it wasn't simply that God had crushed his life dream because of one lousy sin, though granted that would be sick enough—it was that He *knew.* God *knew* He'd never let Moses into the Promised Land, just as He knew that one day Sarah would laugh, but He still let him wander around the desert like a schmuck for forty years searching for it. —*Warmer, warmer, you're getting warmer, you're dead.* God loves that joke. Was that the joke

He had planned for me? Kid gets in a cab to go to the mall on the Sabbath, commits 613 sins, figures he can just make it up by observing the Sabbath next weekend, and God kills him—*ka-blammo*—a four-car pileup, a head-on collision—that very day, in the cab, before he even gets there?

—That *would* be funny, I heard God say.

—I'll get out here, I called again.

The driver turned to face me.

—What? he asked.

—Red light, I said.

—What?

—RED LIGHT!

We shuddered to a stop halfway through the intersection. We were close—I could already see the top of the Nanuet Mall, rising in the distance like the photos I had seen of the Temple Mount in Jerusalem, except instead of a golden yarmulke on its roof, this Promised Land wore a giant inflatable purple dinosaur wearing a banker's cap and smoking a fat cigar. *Come in for Pre-HISTORIC Savings,* read his belly.

I really wanted to live there.

—Here's good, I said.

—You sure?

I got out, closed the door, and waved.

—I'm sure. Here's good.

I went to Spencer's and tried the whoopee cushion. I went to the back of the store and looked at posters of girls in tiny shorts sitting on white sports cars. I stole a package of

Realistic Doggie Doo, and one of the pens with the naked lady inside. After that I went to Waldenbooks, where I sat on the floor with *Physicians' Desk Reference: Guide to Infectious Diseases*. I thought about stealing a *House & Garden* for my mother, but my heart wasn't in it. I was worried. What if God punished sins immediately—what if He didn't wait for you to pay them off? What if she was dead?

I hurried outside and climbed into one of the waiting cabs.

—Carlton Road, I said to the driver.

Two older kids stood on the sidewalk outside the mall. They were smoking cigarettes and taking turns spitting on the floor.

—Fuck this, said one.

—Fuck that, said the other.

—Cool it, said the security guard.

"Black Sabbath," read their T-shirts.

—Funny, I said to God.

By the time we drove past the synagogue, it was already nearly five o'clock, and people were beginning to appear on the side of the road, making their way to afternoon services. I slid down in my seat, afraid someone might see me, and told the driver to keep driving, past the synagogue, to a quieter section farther down Carlton Road. I imagined us driving past my father on his way to synagogue, and I imagined him stepping in front of the cab, waving his arms and shouting for the driver to slow down, and imagined God distracting the driver and making us run him over. There I would be, police cars starting to wail, in the car that struck and killed my father on Sabbath afternoon.

—That *would* be funny, I heard God say.

—Here's good, I said to the driver.

—Here?

—Yeah, yeah. Here's good.

I got out of the cab, stopped at Stone of Pornography (nothing), and headed home. Leon and his friends were in his garage. One of them was holding Leon's BB gun. Leon turned and saw me. I half nodded. He looked away. One of his friends turned his baseball cap around, lifted the gun and pointed it at me.

—Bang, he said.

His friends laughed.

—*Behold,* Rabbi Blowfeld had quoted from Numbers (23:9), —*it is a nation that will dwell in solitude among the nations.* Attempt to dwell in their midst—wear their clothes, go to their malls, ogle their older sisters—bam, Holocaust.

—Beanie boy, the boy said under his breath.

Leon grabbed the gun from him and gave him a shove. He reached up for the garage door. He half nodded. I looked away. Behind me, I heard the garage door close.

—Where have you been? asked my father when I got home, pulling on his suit jacket and tightening his tie.

—Ari's house, I lied.

—Get your brother. You're late for synagogue.

My mother was in the den with the new *House Beautiful.*

—Boy, oh boy, she said. —That's some kitchen.

Her parents had been poor. She had wanted to be a doctor, but her father had taken the money he had saved for her tuition and used it to pay for her older brother's rabbinical education. Soon after she married my father, his father died. He left his entire fortune—millions, I was told—to charity. This wasn't the life she had planned on, and I wondered if that was why she thought about death and decorating so much. Somewhere out there was a better home with my mother's name on it or, failing that, a gravestone. I ran away to the mall, she rearranged the couches. I hoped that greener pastures, and better gardens, lay somewhere ahead for us both, but it made me sad to think that they probably weren't the same gardens, or the same pastures.

—The skylights are nice, I said.

—Not in this life, she sighed.

I found my brother downstairs, who said he didn't want to go to afternoon services, and my father said, —Get your ass in gear, and my brother said no, and my father said, —Don't make me come down there, and my brother said, —I don't care what you do, and my father said, —I'll deal with you later, and told me to follow him and so I did.

I walked beside my father back up the street I had just walked down. At the corner, we passed the Sabbath angels sitting on the ground beneath the dead end sign. They were taking turns flinging pebbles into the nearby sewer.

—Hey, said the first angel.

—Hey, I said.

—How's it going? asked the second angel.

—How do you think? I said.

—So shall it be next Sabbath? asked the first angel.

—So shall it be, I said.

—I hate Sabbath, said the second angel.

—Who doesn't? I said.

We got to synagogue just as the congregation was beginning the *Shemoneh Esreh,* the central prayer of the service. It consists of eighteen separate blessings, and is recited silently, while standing, by each member of the congregation. I grabbed a prayer book from the bookshelf, put my feet together, and began to pray. Afterward, there would be another boring speech by Rabbi Blonsky, then more praying, followed by another *Shemoneh Esreh.* It would be close to forty prayers before the Sabbath was done, but that was just fine with me. I had 613 sins to repay, and six long days until the next Sabbath.

If Mr. Holocaust didn't get me first.

10.

As the obstetrician's nurse pulled on her exam gloves and rubbed conductive gel on Orli's belly, Orli smiled and reached for my hand. I smiled, gave her hand a squeeze, and thought about the first time God tried to kill Moses.

—This is going to be a little cold, said the nurse.

Moses and his wife, Zipporah, were out for a stroll with their son Gershom when a giant serpent swallowed Moses, head first, right down to his waist.

—Is that the baby? Orli asked, her voice almost a whisper, her eyes fixed on the sonogram monitor.

—Sure is, said the nurse.

The serpent quickly released Moses, only to swallow him again, this time feet first. As he had done so earlier, the serpent stopped at Moses' waist.

—Do you want to know? asked the nurse with a grin.

Orli looked at me and shrugged. I shrugged back.

—Okay, she said.

It didn't take long for Zipporah to understand that

Moses was being attacked because they hadn't circumcised their son. She immediately picked up a flint, chopped off her son's foreskin, and the serpent released her husband.

—It's a boy, said the nurse.

Orli smiled at me.

—A what? I said.

—A boy, said the nurse.

—Are you sure? I asked, leaning over Orli to squint at the monitor.

—Oh, I'm sure.

—It looks like a girl, I said.

—You're leaning on my stomach, Orli said to me.

—Been doing this for ten years, said the nurse. —It's a boy.

—Where? I asked. —I don't see anything.

—You're LEANING on my STOMACH, Orli said.

—Sorry.

The nurse pointed to a blurry white smudge on the screen. —Boy, she said with authority. —I can have the doctor come in if you want a second opinion.

—That's okay, said Orli.

The nurse pushed the monitor to the side and stood. —Hoping for a girl, were you? she asked, handing Orli some wipes to clean the gel off her belly. —Boys are easier.

—Maybe, I said. —But you don't have to cut anything off girls.

I'd been dreading this; if I didn't know for certain that God was a prick who spends His time figuring out hilarious ways to screw me over, I might have even *prayed* for a girl, but I knew if I did, He definitely would have given me a boy. I could have tried the reverse-psychology thing—pray for a boy to get a girl—but I was pretty sure He'd see it coming; then He'd give me two boys, twins, just to screw me, and everyone would say, "Oh, what a blessing!" and I'm sure that they would be, but I alone would know the truth, their x's and y's, blessing or not, arranged in malevolence, and then I'd get all pissed off and decide not to circumcise either of them, just to spite the Son of a Bitch, but He'd hear my thoughts and know my plans and He'd make them conjoined twins, connected—ha-ha—by their foreskins, so I'd have no choice but to cut them, and hidden within that punishment, of course, one of those cautionary subtexts He loves so much —*Honor My covenant with Abraham or surely thy children shall piss all over each other all the days of their lives,* or —*If thou shalt not bind them unto Me, I shall bind them unto each other*—a situation that, now that I think of it, would be perfect—not their pissing on each other, but their being connected by their foreskins, because then I'd have no choice but to circumcise them—hell, they'd probably do it right there in the hospital—and then at least *I* wouldn't have to make the decision myself.

The nurse gathered up her papers and headed for the door.

—If it helps, she said, —they don't feel nothing at that age.

—Thanks, I said. —It doesn't.

—I know, she said.

· · ·

—Well, I said to Craig the following morning, —He did it to me again.

—Who?

—*Who*. God, that's Who.

Craig was at his desk. I had slumped down into the corner of the couch on the far side of his office.

—He never gets bored of you, does He? asked Craig. —What now?

—Foreskin, I said.

—Hey! said Craig. —Congratulations!

Craig has two sons, and pictures of them adorn his desktop, his laptop, his iPod, and his cell phone.

I leaned forward and ran my hands through my hair.

—A fucking boy, I said.

—You realize, of course, said Craig, —that there are people out there who can't conceive at all. Who'd be happy with anything.

—That's the problem, I answered. —You have to *not* want something for God to give it to you.

Craig turned back to his computer. I pressed the argument by pointing out that it made perfect sense—people wanting babies not having them, people not wanting them having them without even trying, people wanting boys having girls, people wanting girls having boys, people wanting one having twins, people wanting twins having triplets—if that wasn't proof of the existence of a non-benevolent God, I didn't know what was.

—Do you have the copy for that radio campaign? asked Craig.

I ran my hands through my hair.

—Now I've got this goddamn foreskin thing.

—The client wants it by this afternoon.

I looked up at the ceiling.

—Foreskin, I said to God. —Good one.

Craig is a nice guy, but he was raised with Reform Judaism. Theologically, I have more in common with a Christian.

—If He really wanted to fuck with you, Craig asked, —why doesn't He just kill you?

I scoffed and shook my head.

—Killing gets boring, I said. —A couple of floods and you're over it. Why kill when you can slowly torture?

—I hadn't thought of that.

—That's why He's so into this endless bullshit sniping.

—At you, said Craig.

—Yes, at me. At you, too, you just don't notice it.

An account director walked into Craig's office; Craig was wanted upstairs by the executive creative director, a little man with a big cigar. Craig looked up at the ceiling.

—Good one, he said to God.

I went back to my office and searched the Web for answers. I learned that circumcision was a barbaric ritual. I learned that those who said that circumcision was a barbaric ritual were anti-Semites. I learned that those who said that those who said that circumcision was a barbaric ritual were anti-Semites who were perpetuating an ancient form of child abuse. I learned that in the late 1980s, when Soviet Jews began immigrating in large numbers to Israel, an Israeli newspaper reported that the first thing tens of thousands of them did, young and old alike, was to have a circumcision, lining up all over the Promised Land in assembly-line fashion to undergo the procedure as soon as possible.

—Do you believe in God? the reporter asked an older man who was awaiting his turn.

—No, he replied, —I am an atheist.

The reporter was taken aback.

—Then why have a circumcision? he asked.

The man, fighting back his tears, answered proudly. —Because without a circumcision, he said, —it is impossible to be a Jew!

Orli phoned.

—What are you up to? she asked.

—I'm online, I said. —Checking out foreskins.

—What'd you find?

—An old Russian got one.

—Why?

—Because it's impossible to be a Jew without one. Does that help?

—Thanks, she said. —It doesn't.

—I know.

My family and I are like oil and water, if oil made water depressed and angry and want to kill itself, so Orli and I decided to hire a doula to help us with the birth. Her name was Mary, and she came over a few afternoons later to get acquainted.

—We don't speak to our families, I said.

—That's sad, said Mary.

—Not as sad as when we do, I said.

Mary advised us on doctors and midwives and supplementation, on amniotomy and its relation to umbilical cord prolapse, on the overuse of epidurals and the underuse of perineal massage to avoid unnecessary episiotomies, on the disadvantages of lithotomy and the advantages of prenatal yoga. She advised us to use comfrey for hemorrhoids, to eat organic vegetables over non-organic, to use raspberry tea over black tea, to take generic prenatal vitamins over the more expensive brand-name prenatal vitamins, and recommended the nearby birth center in Rhinebeck over the local hospital in Kingston.

—Where do you stand on circumcision? I asked.

Mary stepped backward and held up her hands.

—That's really your decision, she said.

When Mary had gone, Orli and I went for a hike. We moved to our house in the woods of Ulster County nearly ten years ago. The property backs up on nearly a thousand acres of protected watershed forest, and there is rarely a day that we miss our hikes along the steep, abandoned logging trails and rock-strewn, dried-up creeks that begin just outside our front door. We talk about our work, our hopes, our fears. We resolve arguments, we apologize if we've been wrong, we draw closer together if we've somehow been drawn apart. The trees must be sick of us.

—*Here he goes again with the "mother" talk,* says the maple.

—*I remember,* says the surly old oak, —*when they used to get stoned and* fuck *out here.*

—But what about the Holocaust? I asked Orli that afternoon.

Orli sighed.

—What *about* the Holocaust?

As we walked along an old trail that wound its way up the mountain, I told her the story I'd heard so many times growing up, the story of the old Jewish lady in the concentration camp who circumcised an infant just before its death at the hands of the Nazis. One black evening, the SS had announced that the following morning they were going to kill all the infants in the camp. The old woman began weeping and crying, and she threw herself at the feet of a passing Nazi soldier, begging him for the knife he carried in his belt. The Nazi smiled, thinking that the old Jew wanted to kill herself, and handed her the knife. The old woman fell to her knees and opened the bundle of rags she had been carrying; inside lay an infant boy, and before the Nazi could stop her, she bent over the baby and circumcised him.

—*You have given us a child,* she cried aloud to God, —*and we return to you a Jew.*

It was autumn, and hunting season was a few weeks away. In the distance, someone fired a rifle, and the sound ricocheted off the hills and through the valleys.

—And then what happened? asked Orli.

—I don't know. He killed them, I guess.

We walked along a little farther. Sunlight poured through the tall, dark pines. Another gunshot. Deer looked for their passports; bears begged to hide in their neighbor's attic.

—I don't know what to do, I said. —On the one hand, it's insane; it's mutilation. On the other hand, maybe he should have a connection to his past. On the other hand, I worry God will kill him if we don't do it. On the other hand, I feel guilty not circumcising him when so many Jews in history died for the chance to. I'm like fucking Vishnu here with all these hands.

—Didn't they kill babies every day? asked Orli.

—What?

—It was the Holocaust, she said. —They killed babies every day. It wasn't like, "Okay, today we're killing babies."

Another gunshot, closer this time.

I supposed that they did kill babies every day, but explained that perhaps that wasn't the point. The point was how important this tradition has been to the Jewish people. Then again, isn't tradition just another word for that particularly religious, self-righteous, non-thinking inertia that propels so many to extremes they might not ever have engaged in had they stopped to actually consider, to weigh, to examine? It was treacherous enough, I complained, trying to determine my own beliefs, but here I was being asked to determine someone else's, a someone else that hadn't even developed genitals yet, let alone a philosophy of religion. I mean, what if . . .

—How did she know how to do a circumcision? Orli asked.

—Who?

—The old lady.

—I don't know. It can't be that difficult.

—It can't be that difficult?

Orli's lineage is a physically appealing but discursively frustrating combination of Middle Eastern and Russian; relentless interrogation is in her blood.

—I'm sorry, she continued, —but I'm having a hard time believing this Nazi just *handed* his knife to a Jewish prisoner. A knife is a weapon. And how did she—I mean, you don't just lop it off.

—It was the *Holocaust,* hon.

She kicked a stone down the trail.

—I know it was the Holocaust. I just don't see how rounding people up in concentration camps suddenly makes them all *mohels* [people who perform circumcisions], that's all. Locking me up in Auschwitz isn't going to make me a fucking surgeon.

It was a tense time. We were conflicted about the foreskin, nervous about the baby, and terrified that the introduction of the baby would somehow reintroduce with him the families from which we had worked so long to distance ourselves.

The sun began to set and I called for the dogs, worried

that someone was out there getting an early jump on hunting season. Harley and Duke are Rhodesian ridgebacks, and without their orange safety vests, they look a lot like deer. If I could get one of those vests to protect us from God, I wouldn't even be thinking of circumcising our son.

—I'm sorry, said Orli.

We held hands and headed back down the mountain.

—It's okay.

—Story sounds like bullshit, that's all.

I put my arm around her as we stumbled along the trail home.

I wish she had been there. I wish she had been there when Rabbi Kahn screwed me on the blessing bee. I wish she had been there when I discovered the Stone of Pornography. I wish she had been there in the auditorium on Holocaust Remembrance Day to look over at me after Rabbi Blowfeld told the story of the old lady and the foreskin, and roll her eyes, and mouth the word *Bullshit*.

That's how I know that I love her.

That's how I know I want to be with her forever.

And that's how I know that God is going to kill her.

I took a joint out of my pocket and took a hit.

—I thought you were taking a break, she said.

I shrugged.

I didn't solicit foreskin opinions, but they were offered. It didn't take much:

—Do you know the sex of the baby?

—It's a boy.

And they're off.

Our friend from the posh neighborhood of Brooklyn Heights was in favor of circumcision "for, you know, aesthetically," while my attorney, who is gay, recommended that if we had even the slightest suspicion that our son was homosexual, we just leave the damn thing on.

—They're very prized in my community, he said.

At least someone was thinking of the boy.

I found myself a week later, back in Craig's office, sitting across the way from Patricia, a formerly Orthodox, currently Buddhist, macrobiotic, pro-Palestinian, animal-rights-activist art director.

—I can't believe you're even considering it, she said. —Why don't you just cut off his finger or slice off his nose? Stab him—knife him—for God. That's what you're talking about, isn't it?

I was beginning to feel a bit like a foreskin myself.

—Why don't you just punch him in the face? she suggested as she gathered her papers in an angry pile and started to leave. —Wait eight days, invite the family over, put out some wine and kugel, and just punch him in the fucking face.

A lot like a foreskin. Cut off from my past, uncertain of my future, bloodied, beaten, tossed away. I wondered if there was a place where the foreskins could go, a place where they could live together, peacefully, loved, wanted, a nation of the foreskins, by the foreskins, for the foreskins.

Patricia slammed the door behind her as she left. Craig sat down on the chair across from me.

—Listen, he said.

He took a deep breath and told me that as far as he was concerned, growing up was difficult enough, and that the only reason he had circumcised his own sons was so that they wouldn't wonder someday why they were different from their dad.

—And that, he said, —seemed like a pretty important reason.

I nodded. I liked the whole selflessness angle, but I sighed and shook my head. The fact was, I said to Craig, if I really wanted to ease my son's insecurities by making his penis look like mine, I wasn't going to have to just circumcise him; I was going to have to shave his balls and give him a Prince Albert.

Craig looked at me for a moment before checking his watch.

—I've got a ten o'clock, he said.

11.

*T*he years since the Snack Shack had been filled with secrecy and shame. Vinnie had been right—I couldn't fight the Jimmies. Nor could I fight the Polly-O string cheeses or the Charleston Chews. By nine, overcome by the evil inclination at the Nanuet Mall Food Court, I'd had my first bite of non-kosher pizza. By ten, I was hitting the marshmallows pretty hard. We all know what comes next, and a year later, it did: grilled cheese. —*Sin,* said the Sages of blessed memory, —*leads to sin,* and I took their advice to heart. By the end of the sixth grade, when the rest of the boys wanted to be doctors and lawyers, I wanted to be a Shark. I had just seen *West Side Story* on television, and I was in love with a girl named Maria. Maria wasn't Jewish, but she covered her hair and wore ankle-length skirts. Maybe that would be enough.

—Sir? Sir. Excuse me, sir. I'm going to have to ask your son to empty his pockets.

I was with my father in the parking lot of Caldor's and had just stolen the sound track to *West Side Story.* The security guard stretched out his hand and waited for me to hand him the cassette. My father looked down at me with the opposite of surprise.

—But why? I asked.

—Please, son, said the security guard.

I reached into my pocket and handed him the cassette.

—But why? I asked.

—*Ganif,* muttered my father. Thief.

—But why? cried my mother when we got home.

I didn't know. I knew that she also cried when I didn't steal—cried when she did the bills, cried when I asked for new clothes, cried when my siblings hit her up for allowance.

—*A sound track? Why do you want to waste our hard-earned money on that kind of* narishkeit *[foolishness]? Do you know how long it takes your father to earn that kind of money? You think money grows on trees? You kids are going to put me in the poorhouse.*

I figured it wouldn't suffer the Caldor department store chain to lose a cassette sound track now and then, but it would probably kill my mother to buy one.

She cried that night for a very long time.

—I'm sorry, I said.

—Go, she said. —I can't look at you. Go think about what you've done.

I went to my bedroom, sat on the edge of my bed, and took her advice. —*How the hell,* I wondered, —*did that security guard catch me?* I'd stolen before—Twix, Moon Pies, Three Musketeers—and it was easy: pick up the thing you want, walk around for a little while, pick up other things along the way, put some down, pick some up, put the one you want in your pocket, put the rest down, walk out the door.

How the *hell* did that guy catch me?

I thought and I thought and I thought, and as I thought, I twirled my baseball cap around the tip of my finger—the same baseball cap I had been wearing that night at Caldor's—and that's when it hit me.

—Could it be? I wondered.

I went back to Caldor's a few days later, my baseball cap safely at home in my bedroom closet and, on my head, the biggest yarmulke I could find, pinned prominently to the front of my head. My white *tzitzis* dangled conspicuously from the sides of my pants. Five minutes later, the sound track to *West Side Story* was back in my left coat pocket, and a Hardy Boys paperback was jammed in the right. The same guard that had caught me a few nights ago was once again stationed at the door.

—'Night, I said as I walked toward him.

He had one hand on his gun, the other on his radio, his eyes fixed on a couple of black teenagers heading toward the electronics department.

—'Night, he said without turning to me.

Shark? I was better than a Shark. I was invisible.

Through shops and malls I drifted, seldom seen, never suspected, an angel with overstuffed pockets, a spirit, presumed innocent, the *Bee Gees' Greatest Hits* crammed down the front of his pants. I had thought wearing a baseball cap would make me blend, but now I discovered that wearing a skullcap made me vanish. My yarmulke disappeared me, and, with me, from the beginning of the third grade to the start of yeshiva high school, went albums, comic books, bicycle parts, a three-foot-tall picture frame on the occasion of my parents' wedding anniversary, radios, portable cassette players, toy rockets, toy rocket launchers, and those little packets of three Ritz crackers with the orange slab of non-kosher cheese.

At fourteen, I entered the Metropolitan Talmudical Academy High School on 181st Street and Amsterdam Avenue in New York City. The yeshiva campus was a five-block-long, two-block-wide Brinks-security-protected garrison in the middle of the crime-plagued, drug-infested community near the tip of the island of Manhattan called Washington Heights. By the hundreds we came to this ghetto: from Rockland County, from Queens, from Staten Island, from New Jersey, and from Long Island. We came wearing Ralph Lauren shirts and Girbaud pants. We came wearing Champion sweatshirts and Nike Air Jordans. We came wearing Timberland boots and Avirex leather jackets. I thought people in Monsey were rich until I met people from Westchester. I thought people from Westchester were rich until I met people from Woodmere. I thought people from Woodmere were rich until I met people from Englewood. —*How much richer can they get?* I wondered. Then I met people from Great Neck.

I had been shoplifting from Caldor's for almost six years

now, and I tried my best to remain a loyal non-customer. I continued to steal from them throughout my freshman year, but by the time the tenth grade rolled around, I had to face the fact that Caldor's was simply not prepared to meet the needs of an older, more discriminating shoplifter. I found my father's High Holy Day yarmulke—a dazzling white satin deer-stopper, decorated with silver embroidery and trimmed with gleaming golden thread—draped it over my head, pulled the *tzitzis* strings from my pants, stuck a screw-driver for removing security tags into my pocket, and went to Macy's.

—*Do not,* I said to God as I walked through the store security sensors with a backpack full of stolen clothes, —*fuck around.*

My relationship with God had begun to change. I was tired of the endless spiritual scorecard manipulation, and I imagined God was tired of it, too, tired of the tedious, disin-genuous algebra of penance and sin, and I began to speak with Him as if He were, well, real. Maybe it was all those years of shame and fear. Maybe it was Rabbi Goldfinger telling me so long ago that I was like a forefather heading out on a dangerous journey—hadn't Abraham haggled with God? Hadn't Jacob wrestled with him—kicked His ass, in fact? Hadn't Moses, called upon by God to lead the exodus, told God to find somebody else? They argued, debated, questioned. I scowled, I called Him names, I gave Him the finger. My sentiments may have been a bit more disgruntled and a bit less reverent than those of my forefathers, but they still seemed more respectful to me than the groveling adjuration of the believers around me; at least I was giving Him credit for being able to deal with a little criticism now and then. After all, wouldn't part of being All-Mighty include being All-Self-Examining? All-Open-to-Criticism? All-Honestly-Self-Evaluating? Surrounded as God was by a universe of sycophantic yes-men, perhaps He would appreciate a little honest interaction.

—*Such a dick,* I would say to him when the bus I was running for left without me. —*Honestly, why do You have to be such a dick?*

—*For Christ's sake,* I would say to Him from the pickup window at Pizza Hut. —*It's one lousy pepperoni. You're going to "loathe me in this world and torture me in the next" over a fucking pepperoni? This is why nobody likes You.*

I would frown up at Him if it rained on my parade. I would curse Him if the shit hit the fan. We had extended philosophical debates, often related to the very sin I was committing at the time.

—*I know it's stealing, but come on, they're not going to miss it. No, I don't think that's a facile rationalization, I think it's a reality of the retail environment. It's fucking Macy's—the largest department store in the world, says so right on the door. What do You want me to do, ask my mother for money? You know my mother, You know what my asking her for money does to her. Does that sound facile to You? We're talking real human pain here. You want me to ask her for money? Fine. I'm going to walk out of this store right now with all these clothes stuffed in my backpack. If You want me to ask her, just make the alarm go off, and next time I'll ask her. Go ahead. Let's see. Here I go.*

The alarm never went off.

—*Exactly,* I said to God. —*Dick.*

By sixteen I was hitting bottom, emotionally, criminally, and gastronomically. The guilt was overwhelming. I was popular at school, but my popularity was a tower built on the shifting sand of a thousand empty-calorie lies. With my new driver's permit and my sister's old car, I would cruise the all-night fast-food joints, looking for comfort in meaningless parking-lot orgies of loveless, empty calories. McDonald's, Burger King, White Castle—I'd hit the drive-through and park in a dark corner of the lot, out of the glare of the neon signs and away from streetlights, and I sat there, alone, night after night, defiling myself with two all-beef patties, special sauce, lettuce, cheese, pickles, onions, and a sesame seed bun. (I didn't know what was in the special sauce, but I was pretty sure it didn't have split hooves. Lettuce, pickles, and onions are kosher, but you are required to soak them in order to make sure there are no bugs in them. Bugs are forbidden.)

I told Deena. I had to tell someone.

—But only sometimes, I said. —It's not like I don't eat *any* kosher.

I had loved Deena since the fifth grade. I thought my confession would both assuage my guilt and make me seem dark, troubled, and sexy, like on TV. It did neither. Deena and I were never going to be more than friends, but after I came out to her, we stopped being even that. Maybe it was just life moving on; we were sixteen now and attending yeshiva high school—the phone calls had slowed, and she had made new friends, and when we ran into each other, she seemed uncomfortable.

She'd already heard about the pig.

—It's like you've gone crazy, she said, her voice dropping to a whisper. —Everyone's talking about it. I mean, why are you eating *bacon*?

I wasn't eating bacon—I wasn't *crazy*—but her words dripped with disgust, and instead of shame, I felt, finally, rage.

—*Why?* I asked. —*Why* am I eating bacon?

—Why are you eating non-kosher?

—Why are you eating kosher?

—Because God said I should.

—That's why I'm not.

Deena gasped.

It wasn't really. Then again, maybe it was. Why did I need a reason? Why did I have to be different? Could I really be eating non-kosher just to piss off God?

Not according to my sister.

—You're just doing this to hurt Mom, she said.

A friend of a friend of a neighbor of a friend of hers had seen me leaving a Pizza Hut.

—That's not true, I said. —I'm also doing it to hurt Dad.

My sister gasped.

I wasn't really. Then again, maybe I was. Why couldn't they accept me as I was? Why did my liking something have to mean that I hated someone else? Wasn't it possible that I just loved pig? Why did my enjoyment have to cause so much suffering?

By the time my junior year of high school came around, it was becoming painfully obvious to me that none of the nig-gas in my yeshiva knew shit about motherfucking shit. It was 1987, and I had just discovered rap.

—Did you hurt your leg? my mother asked, forcing a yarmulke on my head. —Why are you limping?

—Why you gotta be like that? I asked.

—Why *must* I be like that, she said. —Now hurry up, you're late for yeshiva. And stop walking around like some kind of *shvartzer*.

I headed out the front door, put on my headphones, took off my shoelaces, and limped up the street to wait for the bus. Rap was a perfect fit; I was at least as angry as the rappers, and I already had a closet full of Tommy and Gir-baud. I didn't always know what they were saying, but I sure liked the way they were saying it.

You and you mind something beatin' from my rhymes
Something something something that I can't find.
I'll something something my gun,
Manuzi[?] weighs a ton,
Because I'm public enemy number one.

Damn straight.

Something wasn't right. I felt, again, like a stranger in a strange land, except the strange land I was in was my own, and the land that wasn't my own seemed less strange than the land I was in. The Girbaud pants didn't help. The Keds didn't help. I felt like the horse on the Polo logo, unsure whether the man on my back with the menacing mallet was God, or family, or community, or all three, but knowing that if I could just throw the son of a bitch, I could run away forever. My attitude toward the world I had come from and my attitude toward the God that I had come from were the same: I was tired, finally, of trying to find favor in someone or Something else's eyes, particularly when that someone or Something seemed to be assholes and/or an Asshole. Our philosophy teacher told us of a man who claimed that God was dead; if only, Friedrich. He was alive, and He was a Prick. Maybe I couldn't run from him—maybe the trip out of the Promised Land was even more treacherous than the one into it—but perhaps, I wondered, I could spoil His sport with simple acquiescence, blithely accepting whatever fate He chose for me—no worrying, no praying, no beseeching, no obsessing. No more bribes, no more payoffs, no more house of worship backroom deals. Radio silence. Not atheism; resignation. So Whatism. Whateverism. Blow Meism. Maybe the forefathers' mistake was answering Him? Maybe they should have just ignored Him? As for the world I had come from—well, I was in Manhattan now, and there was a new world, a better world, a one-dollar subway ride away. The A train station was six blocks away on Fort Washington Avenue, and Times Square was 139 blocks away. I had heard the Washington Heights horror stories: Jews beat up, Jews shot, Jews stabbed, Jews mugged. But once on that train, I was free, onboard a graffiti-covered escape pod to a world I had heard so much nasty shit about I couldn't wait to live there.

> *Something something position, in any condition*
> *Don't get in my way, 'cause I'm something something-ition*
> *I'm proud to be black, and I ain't takin' no crap,*
> *I'm something something-ack, and I'm proud to be black.*

Damn straight.

Grades came easily to me, so I didn't worry about missing class. They gave you a textbook, they asked you to read a certain part of the textbook, they tested you on that certain part of the textbook. Math was a trick; if you knew the trick (cross out the one, carry the two, drop the decimal point, etc.), it was barely a test. Jewish-law tests were the easiest—you simply picked the strictest answer:

A. forgiveness

B. pay a fine

C. pray

D. stoning

Whatever the question is, the answer is D.

I took the A train down to Forty-second Street, went to a few porno shops, took the uptown C back to Eighty-first

Street, crossed the park, and went to the Metropolitan Museum of Art. I walked around the sculpture garden, checked out drawings and prints, stopped by the American Wing, put on my yarmulke, pulled out my *tzitzis,* went down to the gift shop, and stole some books. The main entrance to the gift shop, just off the Great Hall, opens onto the first floor (books, posters, and postcards), but there's a second, smaller entrance upstairs, at the back of the second floor (jewelry, gifts, accessories). The first time I ever stole from there, I picked up a book on Rodin and another on Magritte, a magazine called *ArtNews,* and a box of twentieth-century-masterpiece playing cards. I walked upstairs, smiled at the gift shop employee who was closely watching a black woman near the jewelry counter, and strolled out into European paintings.

Yarmulke. Don't leave home without it.

I enjoyed art, even if, like rap, I didn't know what it all meant. It seemed so wonderfully self-indulgent, so delightfully worthless, World to Come–wise.

It was on one of these trips downtown that I first met José, after cutting class and taking the subway down to Times Square to visit the porno shops.

—Smile, he called to me as I shuffled glumly back from Andrew Blake to *Fiddler on the Roof.* —Can't be that bad.

I was a few blocks from the yeshiva campus. I had just put my yarmulke back on, and José, a jolly, heavyset, middle-aged Hispanic man, was sitting together with some friends on the stoop of a dilapidated old brownstone.

—Worse, I said.

They all laughed.

—I seen some of them rabbis, his friend said. —Look mad as shit.

—You don't know the half of it, I said.

—Come here, said José. He gave me a dime bag, and told me it was on the house. —Name's José.

I nodded, turned, and walked away.

—Hey, kid, he called to me.

I stopped and turned around. José smiled, reached into his pants pocket, and tossed me a free packet of rolling papers.

—Wow! I said. —Thanks, Mean Joe!

They all laughed.

Now we did it every time; the whole transaction—the walk, the swap, the EZ Wider/Mean Joe Greene thing—took less than five minutes. I could leave after Talmud and be back in time for Prophets.

I spent most of my junior year in midtown. I went to the Met, fell in love with de Chirico, and stole books on chiaroscuro and the use of color. I went to MoMA, fell in love with Brancusi, and lifted books on form and meaning. I went to the Guggenheim, fell in love with Giacometti, and pocketed books on representation and man.

I went to the Whitney.

I went back to the Met.

I went to bookstores. I went to the Strand, Rizzoli, Shakespeare & Co. I stole Kafka and Beckett and Pinter and Mamet. I didn't always know what they were saying, but I sure liked the way they said it. In a single afternoon, I could make my way from the European paintings at the Met on Eighty-first and Fifth, to the absurdists at MoMA on Fifty-third and Fifth, to the new releases section at the Triple Treat peep show on Forty-second and Eighth and still be back uptown in time for the afternoon Torah class and the bus back home. The only places I didn't steal from were the porno shops. Yarmulkes didn't fool the porno store owners, who sat on stepladders positioned around the stores—at the ends of the aisles, beside the cash register, beside the front door—and they watched everyone, no matter what they were wearing on their heads. They understood that beneath all the clothes and hats, beneath the pope's mitre and the rabbi's *streimel* and the mullah's *imamah*, we were all the same.

And then, one night, God had enough. I came home from yeshiva to find my mother in my bedroom, sitting on the edge of my bed. She was pale, paler than usual, and her jowls hung low, lower than usual. She held up a McDonald's hamburger wrapper.

—Do you know where I found this? she asked, her voice barely louder than a whisper. My mouth watered.

—McDonald's?

—In your car, she said. —Are you . . .

She could barely bring herself to say the words. A member of the Communist Party? A Nazi? A gay?

—Are you . . . *non-kosher*?

I wanted so badly to tell her—maybe if she could be

okay with me being me, I could be okay with it, too—but I could tell by the way she asked me the question, the way she was disgusted with the very word, that she would never accept me. She would yell, she would cry. She would go Holocaust. *Do you know how many Jews died at the hands of Nazis so you can keep kosher?* Hitler would be mentioned. I would be worse than him. She would tell my father, and he would throw me out of the house. There'd be a scene—my mother yelling at my father—You never encouraged him, Nosson!—my father yelling at me—Not under my roof! Eat your filthy pig somewhere else! I imagined myself living alone in a roach-infested basement apartment in Brooklyn, my days filled with menial, go-nowhere jobs, my nights filled with Filet-O-Fishes and Six-Piece Chicken McNuggets. I could get a futon, maybe some lamps from Ikea, a fern. There's nothing a few gallons of white paint can't fix.

—It's Jeff's, I said. —He's not kosher.

—How could he be not kosher?

I shrugged.

She stood, and she looked at me with great sadness in her eyes. Finally she came close, and for a moment I worried she might hug me and be able to smell the Arby's beef-and-cheddar I washed down with a jamocha shake and curly fries. I knew she didn't believe me, but my mother always preferred a comfortable lie to an uncomfortable truth. She shook her head sadly.

—Those poor people, she said.

A few days later, I drove to Macy's, smoked a joint in the parking lot, and went inside.

—*Don't do it,* said God.

I went to the young men's department, grabbed a handful of clothing, took them into the dressing room, and shoved them into my backpack.

—*It's enough,* said God. —*Don't do it.*

—*Fuck you,* I said to God, and walked out the front door.

—Sir? Sir. Excuse me, sir.

The security guard was running up behind me, one hand on his holster, the other holding up his pants.

—Sir, I'm going to have to ask you to empty your bag.

I had over $500 worth of clothing in my backpack, and a bag of weed in my pocket. A police car wailed in the distance. I had a Talmud test the next morning and a report on Jewish history due later that afternoon.

—*No,* said God. *Fuck you.*

12.

*K*elly was Christian and blond and went to Spring Valley Public High School and had enormous breasts, and so did all her friends, who also were blond and Christian, and they wore tight jeans and played lacrosse, and Kelly drove a Pontiac Trans Am.

Monday mornings, between Talmud class and Prophets, I would sit with Yoni, Yossi, and David in the kosher pizza store across the street from our yeshiva and lie to them.

—A Trans Am! Yossi said. No way!

—Way, I said.

Black, I told them, with the big golden eagle painted on the hood. Yoni drove his father's Mercedes. Yossi drove his father's Mercedes. David sometimes drove his mother's Mercedes, but sometimes he drove his father's Mercedes. Our friend Gideon had just gotten a brand-new Acura Integra GT. Daniel was hoping for a Porsche; after all, his brother had gotten one. I drove my older sister's eight-year-old silver Nissan Pulsar, which, with its trick pop-up headlights, could have been pretty sporty. Unfortunately, the motor on the left headlight had burned out with the light in the popped-up position, and I couldn't get it to pop down. My car looked like Moshe Dayan, the eye-patched Israeli minister of defense.

It was only a minor technicality that the Pontiac Trans Am didn't actually have the big golden eagle on the hood—that was the Pontiac Firebird—but Yoni, Yossi, and David wouldn't know that. They also wouldn't know that Spring Valley High didn't have a lacrosse team. And they would never, ever know, so help me Someone, that the real Kelly wasn't blond.

Real Kelly was brunette. She had big breasts, but as a symptom of her rather serious weight problem, they didn't really count. She clearly had not played lacrosse, or even gone for a brisk walk, in a very long time.

Yoni removed his glasses, wiped his brow, cleaned his lenses with his yarmulke, tucked the wire ends back behind his ears, and leaned across the table.

—Don't leave anything out, he said.

We were seniors at the Metropolitan Talmudical Academy High School for Boys. The Metropolitan Talmudical Academy for Boys had a school for girls. It was a safe 145 blocks away.

That year, after endless requests by Yoni and a group of other sexually frustrated seniors, the rabbis reluctantly agreed to allow the seniors from the boys' yeshiva to organize a one-time chaperoned date with the juniors from the girls' yeshiva. It was small consolation to me. The girls I knew best were pornography stars, ones named Amber and Nikki and Whoppers. The girls from yeshiva were named Miriam and Leah and Pesha and Shainey. They were a mystery to me. First base for them was holding hands, second was a Sabbath walk, third was letting them drive your mother's Mercedes, and a home run was getting engaged. For me, first was anal. Many of the girls were *shomrei negiah,* "watchers of touching," meaning they wouldn't allow a single touch from a man—not a pat, not a tap, not a glancing blow, not even a handshake, not even from their brothers—until the day they were married. They spent their evenings shopping; I spent my evenings locked in my bedroom with a small black-and-white TV, a stolen VCR, and a bag of weed. Just me, Seka, Traci, and the jar of Oil of Olay I had taken from my mother's makeup table. I was depressed and I was lonely, but my genitals never looked younger.

Files beginning with the letter A were placed in a folder marked with the letter A. The folders marked with the letter A were then placed into a file folder marked with the letter A. The file folder was then placed into a file cabinet. The file cabinet was marked with the letter A.

—You're good at this, said the supervisor.

It was Sunday morning, and I was at Good Samaritan Hospital, repaying my debt to society after being arrested and convicted of shoplifting at the Macy's department store in the Nanuet Mall. Along with a tidy fine, I was ordered to perform community service.

—Hi, said Kelly. —I'm Kelly.

I'd never met a Kelly before.

—I'm Steven, I lied.

—They told me your name was Shellum.

—It's both. Call me Steven.

At the beginning of our senior year, my friends and I had each picked non-Jewish names for ourselves. Graduation loomed, and beyond it waited a world of opportunity, a world in which there were, if *Bachelor Party* was to be believed, girls who would touch us. Yoni became John. Yaakov became Jake. Shimon became Simon. It had to be easier for a Jake to get laid than it had been for a Yaakov.

—Shoplifting, I said to Kelly.

—Shoplifting. Kelly nodded. —Me, too. Hey, you like McDonald's? There's one up the road.

I'd been eating non-kosher food for years—Domino's, Friendly's, International House of Pancakes—a secret entrusted to only a few select friends. But I had never openly crossed the meat line, and I had never gone with another person to have a cheeseburger. Even if I had, it wouldn't have been at McDonald's. McDonald's was the most non-kosher place in the world. The only place more non-kosher than McDonald's was Red Lobster, but I didn't need God to tell me not to eat things with antennas. Red Lobster seemed like the place God made you eat as punishment for eating non-kosher in the first place. —*You like* traif? *Here! Eat! EAT* TRAIF!

It was Sunday afternoon, and the parking lot was almost

empty. Aside from the pair of ambulances at the emergency room door idling impatiently for the dying and the dead, the only cars in the lot were a station wagon parked in a no parking zone, my mother's Nissan, which I'd driven to the hospital that morning, and a black Pontiac Trans Am.

—*Please be the Trans Am,* I prayed to God, —*please be the Trans Am.*

It was the Trans Am.

—*You're really coming around,* I said to Him.

The Trans Am was the McDonald's of cars. I yanked open the creaky passenger door and climbed in. Kelly dropped into the driver's seat, the suspension gasped, and Kelly started up the car while handing me a cigarette. I leaned back in my seat, lit up, and hung my elbow out the window. It didn't matter that rust had eaten a hole through the floorboards. It didn't matter that black smoke was coughing out of the Trans Am's exhaust. It didn't matter that just rolling down the window was enough to leave Kelly winded.

Her name was Kelly.

I was smoking a cigarette.

On the way to McDonald's.

In a Trans-fucking-Am.

Kelly ordered a Quarter Pounder with cheese, a Filet-O-Fish, a ten-piece Chicken McNuggets, another eight-piece Chicken McNuggets, a large fries, an apple pie, an ice cream, and a large Diet Coke. I followed her lead, but only so far. I ordered a cheeseburger.

· · ·

Fake Kelly, in my defense, was an accident. Along with my community service, the judge had issued me a heavy fine, which my mother refused to pay.

—But you can't tell anyone what it's for, I said to David.

—Okay, no problem. What's it for?

Jewish-law class had just ended, and we were walking out of the yeshiva, headed for the kosher pizza shop across the street.

—Shoplifting, I said.

—What?

—I was arrested, I told him. —For shoplifting.

David stopped walking. I felt ashamed. It wasn't the worst thing I'd ever done, but it was the worst thing I'd ever done that I'd ever told anyone about.

—Arrested? Are you serious?

I shrugged.

David raised his arms over his head and cheered.

—That is so AWESOME! he shouted. He put his arm around my shoulder and we continued on our way. —Wow! Arrested! You ROCK! What was jail like?

I wouldn't have known. The police were quite friendly. They took my fingerprints, and then they took my mug shots, and then they had me sit on a metal folding chair in an empty holding cell while they waited for some paperwork to return.

—Sorry about the metal, said an officer, it's the only chair we have.

He returned a few minutes later with a padded one. Another officer offered me a Coke, and told me where I could find a candy machine down the hall. —Don't get many Jews, he said. They gave me a lift back to my car at the mall, and I was home an hour later. But I was asking David for a lot of money—$750—and I felt he deserved his money's worth.

—Rough, man, I said. —Really, just . . . rough.

We crossed the street and took a booth in the back of the pizza shop.

—Did they pull their guns? David whispered.

There was no they. "They" was an aging, out-of-breath security guard who had stopped me in the parking lot and asked politely if he could look into my bag.

—One of them did, I nodded. —Big black guy.

—No way, said David.

—Way, I said.

I had been getting around to reading all the books I'd stolen lately, one of which was about how to go about writing a book myself. This was the book I read first. I didn't have much interest in being a writer, but I had a lot of fictions in my life, fictions that covered up some humiliating nonfictions: an obsession with pornography, compulsive stealing, violating Sabbath, eating meat together with milk, walking without a yarmulke. My whole world depended on making my stories believable—encouraging what writers, I had just learned, called "the willful suspension of disbelief"—and I figured I might as well get a few pointers from the professionals.

The twenty minutes on the padded chair in the empty holding cell became eight hours in lockdown with a bunch of strung-out black guys and a neo-Nazi with a swastika tattoo who kept giving me dirty looks. This was what writers called "adding texture."

David shook his head in disbelief. I briefly told David about the hearing, and about the fine, and about the community service. He really liked the part about my having a parole officer, which pleased me, as it was one of the few parts that was actually true. And then, without thinking too much about it, I mentioned Kelly.

—*Kelly*, he said with a smile. —Tell me about *Kelly*.

—She drives a Trans Am, I said. —And she plays lacrosse.

Perhaps, I wondered as I watched David's eyes widen, all creations are accidents. Perhaps God only meant to create some lakes and a couple of birds, but then the birds need trees to really impress them, and the trees need sun, and by day three, things were just completely out of control. An owl here, a mountain there; a week later He's got a whole damn planet on His hands. Some people just don't know when to stop, and I knew how He felt. Over the next twenty minutes, I described Fake Kelly to David in details both large and small—breasts being large, nose being small. She was a parts-bin special of all my favorite adult movie stars, a Frankenstein's hussy: the breasts of Christy Canyon, the hair of Ginger Lynn, the ass of Traci Lords. And a

Pontiac Trans Am. And lacrosse. This is what writers called "characterization."

Yes, maybe I *would* write a book someday. I had always possessed a certain facility with words; when I was very young, my brother teased me so badly that one day I threw a knife at him.

—No, said my mother. —Use your words.

I did. I told him how selfish he was, how he was tearing our family apart with his stubborn belligerence, how he was becoming everything he hated in our father and worse.

—Okay, said my mother, —don't use your words.

David shuffled forward on his seat, and leaned across the table. His eyes burned into mine, waiting for the next chapter. I felt like a television.

This was my life: leave for yeshiva at seven in the morning, home that night by eight, locked in my bedroom by nine, naked by nine-fifteen, and stoned by nine-thirty, blowing pot smoke out the window of my bedroom basement, a Talmud exam the following morning: smoke, masturbate, rinse, repeat, until I was out of porn, out of weed, or just couldn't keep my eyes open any longer. Life probably wasn't any worse for David, but it probably wasn't a whole lot better. We both needed Kelly.

—You do her? he whispered.

I checked over my shoulder. Rabbi Osborn, the vice principal of the yeshiva, sat two booths behind us, buried in a falafel and a greasy copy of *The Jewish Press*.

—Nah, I answered. —But there's always next weekend.

This is what writers called "a hook."

. . .

That Saturday night, after Sabbath ended, I drove to Washington Heights, bought some pot from Jose, and stopped at a nearby newsstand, where I bought some potato chips, a lighter, and a four-hour video compilation of a thousand and one oral sex scenes.

Sunday I saw Real Kelly again.

Files beginning with the letter B were placed in a folder marked with the letter B. The folders which were marked with the letter B were then placed in a file folder that was marked with the letter B. The file folder was then placed into a file cabinet. The file cabinet was marked with the letter B.

—McDonald's? Kelly asked, dangling the keys to her car.

—Sure.

Real Kelly was getting a bit clingy. I wasn't in the mood for McDonald's—last week's burger had given me four days of uncontrollable diarrhea—Yahweh's revenge—but she had, after all, been the inspiration for Fake Kelly, and I felt I owed her for that.

—Sure, I said.

Kelly climbed into the Trans Am. I tossed the empty fast-food bags and soda cups and burger wrappers into the backseat with the rest of the empty fast-food bags and soda cups and burger wrappers, and climbed in beside her.

—I also have to stop at the laundromat. And CVS, over on Route 59.

—No problem.

—There's a White Castle there, too. We can get some dessert.

I sat back in my seat, lit a cigarette, and wondered what Fake Kelly was doing right now. As it turned out, she had been masturbating me in the backseat of her Trans Am.

—No way, said David the next morning.

—Way, I said.

David had told Yossi about Kelly, and Yossi had told Yoni, and the four of us sat huddled in the dark back booth of the kosher pizza shop. Yoni removed his glasses, wiped his brow, cleaned his lenses with his yarmulke, tucked the wire ends back behind his ears, and leaned across the table.

—Don't leave anything out, he said.

I was still on the B folders two weeks later, and Real Kelly was beginning to get on my nerves. I was angry that she wasn't helping out with the filing a bit more, but I was furious that she wasn't more like Fake Kelly, that she wasn't even trying. Fake Kelly carried sex toys and lubricant wherever she went; Real Kelly carried chocolate bars and candy. I sat across from her at Arby's and fumed. It wasn't even her goddamned Trans Am; it belonged to her mother's boyfriend, and since Mama Kelly preferred not to leave the house unnecessarily, she allowed Kelly to drive it in return for her running errands, errands into which I was increasingly roped.

—Mind if we stop at the drugstore?

—I've got to hit Grand Union.

—Just gonna run in to the laundromat.

And always, inevitably, regardless of how late we were, the stop at McDonald's, or Burger King, or White Castle.

—We really should head back to the hospital, I would say.

—You're right, she would answer, pulling into the Wendy's lot. —We'll use the drive-through.

Because of Sabbath, I was able to do my community service only on Sundays, and because of hospital regulations, I was allowed to work only six hours a day. As it was, it would take me four months to finish all two hundred hours, and with Kelly literally eating up half my day's hours, I was looking at the better part of a year before I would have another free weekend.

—Those folders aren't going to file themselves, I said to Kelly.

—Double cheeseburger, Kelly said to the clown sign. —And two apple pies. You want one?

—Sure, I said.

—Make that three, she called to the attendant.

I rolled down my window, lit a cigarette, and wondered what Fake Kelly was doing right now. A car drove by, the driver honked, and Kelly waved.

—What's going on, Kell? asked the girl driving the other car.

—Just getting some lunch, said Kelly. —This is my boyfriend, Steven.

I looked at Kelly, and she smiled.

—*Funny,* I said to God. —*You're a funny guy.*

—She *what?* asked David.

The angrier I became with Real Kelly, the further I progressed sexually with Fake Kelly. The night before, for instance, she blew me.

—No way, said Yoni.

—Way, I said.

It was a leap, but it had been a couple of weeks since the first make-out story, anyway, and my audience seemed to be getting impatient. I needed to keep the story going. This is what writers called "the dreaded second act."

For a few moments, nobody spoke.

—How? asked Yossi.

It was a "how" of disbelief, an existential "how," a howl of a "how," a "How can God allow a thing like this to not happen to me?"

It had, after all, been a wild night. I had been partying with Kelly and her friend Jill. Everything was kind of cool until their friend Sabrina came over; only later did it occur to me that I had named all my characters after *Charlie's Angels.* I based my Kelly stories on scenes from porno movies I had watched the night before—this is what writers called an "homage"—adding particular emphasis on the things, like the Trans Am, which had tested well with audiences in prior stories: Sabrina came over, and we got in the

Trans Am; we drove the Trans Am to a drive-in movie, where we parked the Trans Am; and Jill and Sabrina were in the backseat of the Trans Am, and Kelly was wearing this really short skirt, and one thing led to another and . . .

—A drive-in? asked Yoni.

—Yeah, I said.

—There are still drive-ins?

—Sure.

—Wow! said David. Right in front of Jill and Sabrina! I nodded sagely.

—Where are there drive-ins? Yoni asked.

—Just up the road from me, I said.

—I haven't seen a drive-in in years, said Yoni.

—Do you want to hear about drive-ins or blow jobs? I snapped.

—Blow jobs, said David.

—Yeah, said Yossi. —Blow jobs.

—Because we can talk about drive-ins if you want to talk about drive-ins.

—No, no, said Yoni. —Let's talk about blow jobs.

Rabbi Osborn walked into the pizza shop and pointed to his wristwatch. Five minutes to Prophets. I stood to leave, and David punched Yoni in the arm.

—Nice going, he said.

Files beginning with the letter C were placed in a folder marked with the letter C.

—Her name? I asked. —Her name is Sabrina.

Kelly had heard it all before.

—How long have you been going out with her? she asked.

—We've been friends for a while, I said.

Kelly shrugged.

—That's always the best way, she said.

—Yeah, I said. —I'm sorry.

She shook her head.

—Nah.

—We'll always have McDonald's, I said.

She smiled and jiggled her car keys.

—Nuts, she said, peering into her purse. —You mind stopping at my place to pick up some cash?

—Not at all.

We climbed into her Trans Am and drove to an area that, despite my living twenty minutes away for the last eighteen years, I'd never seen before. Gone were the well-manicured lawns of my neighborhood, and the two-car garages and swimming pools and well-kept lawns. There were no lawns, only large patches of dirt and weeds, riddled with rusted bicycles, rusted fridges, and rusted cars, as if the whole driving force behind capitalism were the struggle to resist rust; here rust was winning.

Kelly parked in front of a small trailer home, its front porch piled high with bags of garbage and twisted lawn furniture.

—Be right back, she said.

A bed frame leaned against the side of the house, its mattress on the ground nearby, collecting water. An empty stove sat beside an old truck, and I thought of my mother, thirty miles away, sitting in our four-bedroom split-level ranch on one and a half acres, complaining about money.

We went to McDonald's. I paid. We laughed a lot and I put my arm around her and felt like a hero.

My mother was waiting for me at the front door. She saw me and slowly held up a cigarette butt she had found in my room.

—What about it? I asked.

—Is this a marijuana stick?

—A marijuana stick?

—You know what I mean.

—You mean a joint?

—Is it?

—No.

—What is it, then?

—It's a cigarette butt.

—Ha! And why, exactly, should I believe you?

—Because it says Marlboro on the side. And there's a filter on it.

She angrily threw the butt on the floor.

—We're sending you to Israel, she said.

—I'm not going to Israel.

—The hell you're not.

I pushed past her and went inside.

—The hell I am.

It is something of a custom for Orthodox Jewish teenagers to spend the year after high school studying Torah in Israel, for which they will receive eternal rewards in the World to Come and, if all the proper paperwork is filed, a limited number of college credits toward a select number of universities.

—I don't even know who you are anymore, she spat.

I went to my bedroom, locked the door, rolled a marijuana stick, and took out my four-hour compilation of oral sex scenes. *Pictures do not represent actual contents,* read the box cover. The same thing could be said for my whole stupid life.

So I lost my virginity.

—No way! said David.

—Way.

We were all on the sidewalk, waiting for the next class to begin. David hugged me. Someone slapped me on the back.

—Too bad, said Yoni. —I had the perfect girl for you.

Yoni was in charge of the senior/junior date. It was his job to match the seniors from the boys' school with juniors from the girls' school.

—Really? I asked. —Who?

—Becky Jacobowitz, said Yoni.

Becky Jacobowitz was the sluttiest girl in the whole yeshiva. She was the only slut in the yeshiva. She once had a boyfriend who was in college. Even her initials were BJ.

God began to chuckle.

—I can still go, I said. —It's not like me and Kelly are *married*.

Yoni shook his head.

—Becky knows you're going out with Kelly.

God was laughing now, wiping tears from His eyes and slapping His knee.

—Kelly's fine with it, I said.

David clapped his hands. —I have got to meet this chick, he said.

Yoni shook his head. —I don't think so.

The first bell rang for Jewish history, and Yoni and Yossi headed inside. David stayed behind and turned to me.

—I was serious, said David.

—Serious about what?

—Introduce me.

—To who?

—To Kelly.

—Kelly?

—I need to have sex, said David.

—With my girlfriend?

—You said it was okay.

—Not to have sex with her.

—What about Jill?

—David, Jill's dating someone.

—How about Sabrina?

I sighed.

—Sabrina's a mess, Dave. She, you know, she does a lot of coke. And she sleeps around, I mean, a lot. And not in a good way. And her ex-boyfriend's crazy. Charlie. He'd kill you. I'm serious.

The second bell rang. Rabbi Osborn stepped outside, pointed to his watch, and waved us in.

—I loaned you a lot of money, said David. —You owe me.

I sighed. After a few moments, I nodded. David slapped me on the back, gave me the thumbs-up, and headed back inside.

In the past two days, I had broken up with a real girl, had sex with a fake girl, ruined an opportunity to go out with another real girl, and agreed to introduce my friend to a girl who didn't even exist.

This is what storytellers call "the complication."

God rolled on the floor and held His sides.

Files beginning with the letter D were placed in a folder marked with the letter D.

—Where's Kelly? I asked the administrator.

Here was my plan: I patch things up with Kelly, get her to lose a few pounds, ask her to dye her hair blond, hang out at McDonald's with her a bit, meet some of her friends, and see if any of them were interested in having casual sex with my friend who was an Orthodox yeshiva student. It was a long shot.

It had been two weeks now since Kelly had shown up at the hospital, and there was just so long I could stall David.

—Kelly won't be joining us anymore, said the administrator.

For certain convictions, he explained, enrollment in a religious institution counts toward community service. Kelly's conviction was one of them. Two weeks ago, she had checked herself into a nearby Christian seminary.

—Not to worry, the administrator said. —You won't be too lonely, though. They're sending another little criminal over next weekend.

—*Make her hot*, I prayed to God. —*I'll do whatever you want.*

—Not now, I snapped at David.

We were standing on the corner of 181st Street, and he was pestering me about meeting Sabrina.

—I need sex, he said to me.

—So do I.

—You? You get all the sex in the world.

Pictures do not represent actual contents.

—Not anymore, I said.

I didn't want to kill off Fake Kelly; I had come to like her. She was nice to have round. Nice to believe in. A Promised Land we could all talk about and imagine, something to get us through the slavery of the day. It was more than just sex. It was hope.

—We broke up.

—No way.

—Way.

I sighed. Things hadn't been working out. We'd been

bored for some time. Sabrina made a pass at me. Jill wanted
a three-way. Kelly didn't want to see me again.

—Love dies, I said.

—Unbelievable.

—I'm okay.

—A three-way!

I kept to myself the rest of the day and let the story make
its way around. I ran into Yoni after the final bell.

—Sorry, he said.

—Becky Jacobowitz? I asked.

He put his arm on my shoulder and nodded.

Two weeks later, I found myself parked with BJ Jacobowitz
in the driveway of her parents' home at one o'clock in the
morning. I stared down at the Star of David between her
breasts, put my arm around her, and pulled her close. We
hugged. I could feel her hair on my face. I could smell the
perfume from her neck. I could hear her crying.

—What's wrong? I asked.

She pulled away from me and covered her face with her
hands.

—I'm afraid.

—What?

—Of you, she said. —You're so . . . experienced.

—What?

—I've heard.

God began to chuckle.

—I'll go slow.

—No, she said. —I can't.

I looked out the window and shook my head.

—But . . . I heard the same thing about you, I said.

Becky burst into tears.

—I made it all up! she cried.

There had been a boyfriend, yes, but nothing had ever happened; the nothing was the cause of the breakup. When the girls at school started saying she had gone all the way, she liked the way it felt, liked the way the others looked at her. And so she never quite mentioned that she and her boyfriend had broken up, or that they hadn't quite done anything with each other, or, for that matter, that he was in yeshiva college.

—No way, I said.

—Way, sobbed Becky.

I'd been picturing the quarterback for Duke.

This is what writers called "irony."

We sat there silently for a moment, nothing around us but the sounds of the engine's impatient hum and God's hysterical laughter.

—I can't believe you're telling me the truth, I said.

—I know, she whined.

I meant it as a compliment.

I tried again to convince Becky we would go slowly, that experience in this field was a benefit, not a drawback.

—Look, if you want me to fumble around clumsily with your bra hook, I will; I'm just saying, I don't have to.

But it was no use.

—I'm not like that, said Becky.

Kelly wasn't like that, either. Nobody was like that. I was beginning to suspect that pornography was lying to me.

I told Becky it was okay. I told her I lied about some things, too. We sat together for a while, talking about friends and school, and then I walked her to her front door and kissed her good night, and we hugged, two lonely liars in the harsh, accusing spotlight of the moon.

Files beginning with the letter E were placed in a folder marked with the letter E. The folders marked with the letter E were then placed in a file folder marked with the letter E. The file folder was then placed into a file cabinet. The file cabinet was marked with the letter E. Later that day, I phoned my parole officer and asked if she had ever heard of enrollment in a religious institution counting as community service. I drove home and found my mother in the kitchen.

—Mom?

We didn't talk much those days, didn't even look at each other much.

—Mmm, she said.

—I think some time in Israel would do me good.

She looked up at me, smiled, and took my face in her hands.

—Blessed is God, she said.

13.

*E*arly in Orli's third trimester, I came home from work to find a message waiting for me on the answering machine. It was from my mother.

—Hi, kids. I just wanted to see how Orli was feeling. If you need the name of a *mohel,* let me know. He's by us, but maybe he knows somebody up there. There must be someone up there who does it. I know someone who had a friend in Tannersville, and they just had someone up there do their son. I can get you the name, if you want. Unless you're doing it down here, near the city, that might just be easier, I have a thousand people here that can do it, so just let me know.

This was what I had dreaded from the beginning. My family had gotten inside again, shots had been fired, and the bullets ricocheted around the once-secure walls of my life until a week or so later one struck me in the back of my head and I fell, bleeding, and crawled my way to my psychiatrist and said, —I'm hit.

—Why don't you write about it? he asked.

Three hundred fifty dollars an hour.

—I'm worried, I said. —We have no photos in our house. We have photos of ourselves, as adults, but there are none of our parents, none of our childhoods. It's like Adam and Eve's house; we came out of nothing.

—I don't follow.

—They were born as adults.

—Right.

—Adam and Eve at Niagara Falls, Adam and Eve at the Grand Canyon. But no kindergarten photos on the walls, no baby pictures.

—Probably hard to find frames back then.

—What if he asks?

—Who?

—Our son.

—Why don't you write about it?

—"Dear Son, Here's why the walls are bare"?

—Sure.

Three hundred fifty dollars an hour.

I went back to the agency and began flipping through stock photography catalogues.

Dear Son,

I probably shouldn't even be doing this. I'm probably going to get you killed. If God hears about this, we're both fucked. Here's what my mother looks like:

That's not an actual photo. It's a stock photograph. People take photos and sell them to advertising agencies to use in ads. I work in an advertising agency. Yeah, I know. But see that pool in our backyard? Anyway, here's another one that looks like her:

I don't know what she's crying about, but I'm pretty sure it has to do with me. Maybe I had a cheeseburger. That's a complicated joke, but for now, let's just say that my mother really hated cheeseburgers. She hated them so much she didn't want me to eat

them. But I did. And now we don't talk. Here's one
that looks like my father:

Here's another one:

Someone must have just told him a joke.

I'm very conflicted about all this, son. I worry
that God will punish me somehow. For talking, for
spilling the beans, for disrespecting my parents, for

pride, for arrogance. The obvious thing for Him to do would be to kill you. Or He could kill Mommy. Here's the kind of school I went to when I was young:

That was recess.

Me and this God go way back, and I'm waiting to find out that He's got something really earth-shatteringly tragic planned, that every day that passes without a death is part of an extremely long setup to some colossally evil joke, one that won't play out until I'm old and it's too late to change anything and I have to live with my pain and shame until I die. Here's what they told me God was like:

I know it doesn't make sense. I know I shouldn't believe it. I know, and I know, and I know, but I just can't seem to get this Character out of my head. I've tried to forget, I've tried to reframe Him, to rewrite Him, to move on. I read Sam Harris. I read Richard Dawkins. It all makes sense, but none of it *helps*. Maybe I'm beyond help. I still worry—I worry that against all logic there is a God, and I'll die and the angels will take me by my arms, and we'll ascend to heaven and the doors of heaven will open, and the angels will sing, and the rams' horns will blow, and there He will be:

That was as far as I got.

—*I'm stopping now, okay, You Pain in the Ass?* I said to God. —*I'm stopping. Relax.*

Then I deleted the file.

Are you sure, the computer asked me, *you want to remove the items in the Trash permanently? You cannot undo this action.*

I was sure.

I drove home that day in a fog. I had spent twelve years trying to eke out some space for myself, trying to build a family where I was loved for who I was, and not hated for what I wasn't, and I had just begun to succeed, a success that led to joy, a joy that led to a baby, and a baby that now threatened to bring that family crashing right back into my life. And with me, always, like venereal disease, the Lord.

At a traffic light, I pulled up alongside a tractor-trailer belonging to a shipping company. The company was named Guaranteed Overnight Delivery. There on the sidewall, in ten-foot-tall red letters, was their acronym: G.O.D.

—*Good one, God.*

Prick.

14.

*T*his is how we came that year, eighteen years old and alone, from New York and Los Angeles and Chicago and Florida, from the cities and from the suburbs, to the Middle East, to Israel, to the Promised Land, the land of our forefathers, the "land which I will show you," looking for what we thought was God: we came with hockey sticks. With Nike Air Jordans and Avirex leather jackets and Rollerblades. With *Hustler*s and *Penthouse*s and *Playboy*s. We came with Oakley sunglasses and Sony Walkmans and cartons of American cigarettes.

Before I left, my mother had told me how she remembered her family sitting around the radio—she wasn't more than ten years old at the time—holding their breath as they listened to the UN tallying votes on the matter before them concerning the creation of the state of Israel. She told me how her father had cried and how, years later, when her brother had become a successful rabbi, he flew his father to Israel for the very first time. Already an older man, my grandfather stepped carefully off the airplane, began to cry, and fell to his knees, kissing the ground and reciting the Shema: *Hear O Israel, the Lord your God, the Lord is One.*

The doors of my El Al jet opened. The air was too hot to breathe.

—Fuck me, I said.

I took shallow breaths, letting them cool in my mouth a moment before taking them deeper into my lungs. The sun burned down upon the land with the vengeance of a furious God. Not like. With.

Sol nudged me, and pointed to a *chayelet,* a female IDF soldier, standing at the bottom of the airway stairs. Her bronze skin glistened in the sun and her biceps rippled as she shifted her Uzi to her other adorable shoulder.

And God tested Abraham.

—Fuck me, I said.

—I know, said Sol. —Sweet.

Four words, two curses. And I hadn't even gotten off the plane yet.

Jerusalem is the holiest city in all of Israel, home to King David's Tomb, the Temple Mount, the Wailing Wall, and the Mir Yeshiva, filled with thousands of students studying Talmud, Torah, and rabbinical literature. Tel Aviv is the unholiest city in all of Israel, home to nightclubs, strippers, hookers, and Bar-Ilan University, filled with thousands of students studying humanities, life sciences, social sciences, and non-rabbinical literature. Our yeshiva, Neveh Zion (Village of

Zion), was in a small town named Telshe Stone, halfway between Tel Aviv and Jerusalem. Left to heaven, right to hell.

Telshe Stone was a hill, nothing more, with a single market, a ritual bath, and a yeshiva for wayward Jewish teens at the top. The design of the town seemed roughly based on the receiving of the Ten Commandments at Mount Sinai: the yeshiva above, and the town, what there was of it, huddled below. Every morning, the rabbis would trudge up Baal Shem Tov Street (named after a famous rabbi) to study the word of God. At the bottom of the hill, Baal Shem Tov Street crossed Marcus Street (named after a famous soldier), and there, at the intersection of Rabbi and Soldier, is where taxis and the occasional bus to Jerusalem would pick up and drop off their passengers.

—Here, said our taxi driver that first day, as he pulled to a stop in front of the security gates.

—Here? I asked.

—Here.

—Where here? asked Sol. —Yeshiva here?

—Up, said the driver. —Up.

—Can you drive us up? I asked him.

He caught my eye in the rearview mirror and smiled sheepishly as he shook his head.

—*Aravi*, he said in Hebrew. Arab.

Sol punched me in the arm and held out his hand.

—Pay up, he said.

We had gotten into a debate outside the airport. We had been warned for months before never to get into an Arab cab, but couldn't remember which were the Israeli cabs and which were Arab; Sol said Israeli taxis had the yellow license plates and the Arab taxis had the blue license plates. I insisted it was the other way around.

—Blue is the national color, you idiot, I argued. —Why would they give the Arabs blue plates?

—Blue is depressing, said Sol. —Yellow is happy. Arab cabs are depressing, Jewish cabs are happy.

I paid the driver, gave Sol twenty shekels, and we headed up the hill. I was depressed. Sol was happy.

There were dozens of American religious schools in Israel, each occupying a slightly different position along the piety scale. The House of Study for Torah was middle of the scale, Yeshiva of the Wailing Wall and Gates of Jerusalem were more pious than that, and Candle of Israel was holier than them all. All of these schools had strict rules, long schedules, and high expectations. Neveh Zion was at the bottom, with no rules, no set schedule, and no expectations.

The yeshiva prided itself in bringing troubled Jewish teens back into the fold. Half the students weren't religious at all, and came from broken or troubled homes. The other half were already religious, and came for the loose rules and "go at your own pace" philosophy.

The yeshiva was an unfinished building originally built for other owners who had abandoned the building in mid-construction, when they ran out of money. The main study

hall was unfinished, with windowless windows in the walls
and huge holes in the roof. Birds flew in and out during the
summer, and nested in the eaves during winter.

When we arrived at the top of the hill, we made our way
to the dormitory, where a student named Winreb was standing on the edge of the roof and threatening to kill himself.
This never would have happened at Candle of Israel. On the
ground below Winreb, a scrawny, gleeful British rabbi—I
would find out later his name was Rabbi Wint—was trying
to talk Winreb down.

—Stop messing about, called Rabbi Wint.

—I'm going to jump! shouted Winreb.

—You're going to miss lunch!

Winreb peered over the edge. —What is it? he called.

—Schnitzel, called Rabbi Wint.

Sol and I had dragged our bags up the front steps and,
exhausted, stopped to watch.

—Jump, called Sol.

Rabbi Wint turned and saw us, and began clapping his
hands and jumping up and down. —More students! he
sang. —More students to study the word of Hashem!
Blessed is God!

Winreb leaned over the edge of the roof and frowned.

—Who are they? Winreb called to Rabbi Wint.

—Don't lean! called Rabbi Wint.

—Sol, called Sol.

Rabbi Wint started clapping again, and began singing
"Blessed are those who enter in the Name of God."

—Who are you? Winreb called to me.

—Shalom, I called, throwing a bag over my shoulder and heading inside. —I've got the roof next.

Rabbi Wint stopped singing and grabbed me by my arm. —Auslander? he asked.

I nodded.

—You have to go to Rabbi Grunther's office, he said.

Rabbi Grunther was the principal.

—Why?

—Come, come, he said, pulling me by the arm.

—But I've got next . . .

Four IDF F-16s passed overhead in tight formation. The American students cheered.

Inside Rabbi Grunther's office, a man from Interpol was waiting to speak with me. He asked me if I had informed my parole officer that I was leaving the country.

—Of course, I said.

—Parole officer? asked Rabbi Grunther.

—Your passport came up under parole, said the Interpol officer.

—I told her months ago, I said. —Call her.

—Parole officer? asked Rabbi Grunther.

—We'll have to call her from my office, said the Interpol officer. He turned to Rabbi Grunther. —We'll bring him back when we straighten this out.

—Parole officer? asked Rabbi Grunther.

I was back at the yeshiva a few hours later, and Winreb was still on the roof.

—Still haven't gotten him down? I asked a Canadian student named Moshe.

—They did, said Moshe. —He went back up. Grunther's looking for you.

I found Rabbi Grunther in his office. He closed the door and lit a cigarette. After offering me one, he sat heavily in his chair and leaned forward on his desk.

—I don't need you to go to classes, he said.

—I know.

—I don't need you to go to services.

—I know.

—But if I catch you with drugs—if I even hear a rumor of drugs—you're out.

—I know.

He took a long drag off his cigarette and squinted at me through the smoke.

—What were you arrested for? he asked.

—Shoplifting.

—What did you steal?

—Clothes.

He nodded.

—Why? he asked.

I shrugged. He had already asked me more about it than my mother ever had.

He invited me to his house for Friday-night dinner, and I accepted. All the rabbis lived in town, and every Friday night and Saturday afternoon, they would generously invite students—five or six at a time—to their homes to share in the meals their wives had cooked. These were often families of seven or eight, with barely enough money to feed themselves, offering their food to American students whose parents earned more in a day than they earned in a year. They weren't doing this out of the kindness of their hearts; they were doing it to make us more religious. Strict rules and regulations had failed to make any of us observant, that was why we were here. So the rabbis at Neveh took the emotional route, filling the void left by our dysfunctional families in order to "bring us back." In the process, of course, they were neglecting their own families, but all of their suffering would be repaid with unfathomable rewards in the World to Come. I knew it was manipulative and I knew it was selfish, but coming from New York, I was fascinated to see someone care about something more than money.

I went back to the dorm. Winreb had come down from the roof. Inside, the arriving students were busy unpacking their duffel bags and hanging pictures on their walls. The first-year students hung posters of sports cars, body builders, and fashion models. Second-year students—the saved, and soon to be saviors—hung pictures of the Temple Mount and photographs of famous rabbis: Rav Shach, Rabbi Feinstein, the other Rabbi Feinstein. Rabbi Wint was shuffling from room to room, welcoming students and rushing them off to prayers.

—Ach! he shouted as he came into my room, covering his eyes and turning his head.

—What? I asked.

—You have to take that down, he said, pointing to a poster of Cindy Crawford I had hung above my bed.

—Why?

—Why? Because she's naked.

—She's in a bikini.

—You like her, don't you? my roommate said to him.

—I don't even know her, said Rabbi Wint.

We all laughed. Rabbi Wint still hadn't uncovered his eyes.

—If you don't take it down, he said, —I can't come in here anymore.

—How's that a problem for me? I asked.

Wint laughed.

—A *talmid chuchum*! he said. A wise student. He went back into the hall, chasing after other students. —Dovid! It's time for *Mincha*! Chaim! Let's go! God is waiting!

I went to the doorway and leaned against the frame, watching as Rabbi Wint rustled up as many students as he could find and marched them across the yard to the prayer hall. To heaven they went, in blue New York Rangers jerseys and yellow Pittsburgh Penguins jerseys and pin-striped Yankees baseball caps and red Nike sneakers. Winreb peeked out from behind some bushes and dashed past me, up the stairs, toward the roof again. A first-year student named Doni was standing outside in the sun, wearing his leather hockey gloves and helmet, practicing his wrist shot against the wall of the dorm. On the front steps, a student named Dovid was making a bong out of a Maccabee beer can.

—You hooked up? I asked him.

He shook his head and shrugged.

—Just in case, he said.

I nodded.

—Second year? I asked him.

—Yup.

—Why did you come back?

He smiled and held out his arms, indicating all that was around him.

—Or stay home? With my parents?

I nodded again.

Rabbi Wint waved to us from across the way. —Hashem is waiting! he called.

I went back to my room, locked the door, closed my eyes, thought about the *chayelet* at the airport, and defiled us both.

Day One.

Rabbi Freidman had dropped a lot of acid.

—I could roll a joint with one hand while riding a bicycle, he told us.

It was on an acid trip that he had picked up God; he'd had a vision of the Eternal One and seen the error of his ways. Somehow he found his way to a yeshiva and never left. That had been fifteen years earlier. Rabbi Marcus had been in a street gang, then an officer in the Israeli army. Most of the rabbis at Neveh had such stories, and they told them proudly to gatherings of students. These stories were meant to be inspirational; I saw them as cautionary.

I spent my first few months in the Holy Land of my fore-fathers getting drunk and trying to find a pot connection. Israelis sold pot, I was told, and Arabs sold hashish; I didn't know what hope there could possibly be for the Middle East if they couldn't even agree on how to get high. Hebrew University students were the ones to go to for mushrooms and, if one was so inclined, there was always Haifa, a central distribution center for the international heroin trade. All I'd ever heard about was the milk and honey.

It was two full months before I stepped into the prayer hall, and three before I attended a prayer service. Even then I made sure to be stoned, and I stood in the back of the room, by the door, and left as soon as the rabbi began his speech.

I had reason to be concerned: my friends had picked me as the one to "wig out." We all knew people who had come to Israel for the year in "Frankie Says Relax" shirts and gel in their hair and returned home ten months later with a complete set of the Talmud in their bags and black fedoras on their heads. Some of them returned for a second year, some for a third, some never left, a terrifying upward spiral that seemed to have no end, and I wasn't taking any chances. Partially to protect myself, partially for the free beer, I took a night job tending bar at a small pub in Jerusalem, pouring Maccabee beer for Israeli soldiers and American yeshiva students. It was there that I first met Naomi.

Naomi was a religious girl from a religious family in Long Island, a friend of a friend of a friend of mine named

Tzvi. I was in Israel running out the clock on a shoplifting conviction, she was there to experience a closer connection to her people and her God. Sparks flew. Naomi ordered a Diet Coke, her friend Rachel had a glass of water, and they coyly invited me to join them the following day for a trip to the Wailing Wall.

The Wailing Wall is the holiest place in all of Judaism save for the Temple Mount itself, the last remnant of the Second Temple destroyed by the Romans in the year 70 C.E. Ever since, Jews have come to the wall to pray and to wail and to cram handwritten notes to God in the narrow spaces between the enormous Herodian boulders of which the wall is built. It is said that prayers left here are the first to be answered by God, and so the crevices of the wall are packed tight with petitions for health, happiness, forgiveness, a cure, a windfall, an answer, a sign, a gruesome gray grout of helplessness and despair.

I'd been avoiding the damn place ever since I arrived. I'd heard of people having breakdowns, of sobbing, of crying, of non-believers believing, of one guy who decided he was the prophet Jeremiah and could speak with God, of a second who claimed to be Ezekiel, of a third who decided he was King David and had been sitting at the wall ever since, in a shimmering white robe, strumming a plastic gold-colored harp.

I declined their invitation.

All the good prophets were taken.

· · ·

January.

Ari had some Arabs who wanted Air Jordans. He was asking 300 shekels for the pair, about $150, twice what he had paid for them back in New York, but you couldn't get them here, not even in Tel Aviv. Ari had a suitcase full of them, another full of Rollerblades, and a closet full of pornography magazines he rented out to other students for a shekel a night. Should the magazine be soiled, manipulated, or in any other way deemed unusable by future customers, the renter was responsible to pay the entire cover price of the magazine, plus an additional fee to cover Ari's trouble in bringing the porn over from America.

The Arabs had come to the yeshiva, but they were looking for a trade.

—I don't want nothing you got, Ari said, and laughed.

I did. I gave them forty shekels and met them an hour later at the bottom of the hill.

I'd never smoked hash before. I went out back with Moshe, Dovid, and Dovid's Maccabee beer can bong, and we sat on the edge of the unfinished in-ground pool. Islamic prayers floated across the valley from the loudspeaker of a nearby mosque. Dovid took a hit, grimaced, and shook his head.

—Camel shit, said Dovid.

—You sure? I asked.

This was where the guidance of the second-year students really paid off.

Dovid nodded.

—Ugh, said Moshe.

—Camel shit, said Dovid, wiping the back of his hand across his mouth.

For some reason, I thought of Naomi. I imagined her in some pristine white dormitory, making challah or polishing her Sabbath shoes. Something pure, something simple.

I took my camel shit and went inside.

Geographically speaking, Israel has only two seasons: Holy Crap It's Hot, and Holy Crap It's Cold. Holy Crap It's Cold lasts from December to March, and the rain never ceases.

—Shalom, someone shouted late one Feburary night. I was in my dorm room, trying to figure out how to huddle underneath my covers and still smoke a cigarette. —Phone!

Doni's mother sent candy, cases of it. A week after the candy arrived, the cakes showed up—cookies, brownies, Rice Krispies Treats. David's mother sent checks. Seth's mother sent clothes—an Izod shirt, socks, thermals. My mother phoned me every two weeks full of poorly disguised inquiries into the current state of my highly anticipated religious transformation, each question sent aloft like a dove from Noah's Ark, filled with the hope of some joyful news upon their return: what were the rabbis like, what was I studying, had I been to the Wailing Wall or the Holocaust Memorial or the ancient burial place of Abraham and Sarah.

—*Not today,* I wanted to say. —*I was going to go, but I spent the last of my weekly allowance on a bag of camel shit. Arab guy sold me camel shit, Mom, you believe that? We can't even deal drugs with one another. Was Camp David completely for naught?*

—It's Baba, said my mother. My grandmother.

When I was younger, Baba gave me non-kosher Chiclets chewing gum.

—Ma, complained my mother.

—They're just kids, said Baba.

Before I left for Israel, I visited Baba one last time, knowing she would likely succumb to Alzheimer's before I returned. I'd sat there beside her bed, holding her hand and trying to comfort myself with the thought that her mind had already died some time ago. When that didn't work, I told myself that it was all for the best. When that didn't work, I cried, said, —Bye, Baba, and hurried out the door.

—Maybe you could go to the Wailing Wall, my mother said. —Say a little prayer for her.

She'd been waiting a long time to drop that one. The atomic bomb of guilt: dead Mommy.

—Man plans, she sighed in Yiddish, —and God laughs.

I could hear Him now.

I lay quietly in bed for some time, staring at Cindy Crawford and wondering what to do. *Man plans and God laughs.*

What kind of a stupid fucking aphorism is that? You mean He's a dick? What ever happened to *Man plans and God does His best to bring those plans to successful fruition?* What religion had that expression? Tell me something, Cindy—man plans, God laughs . . . now go to a wall and pray to Him? Why? If He was half the Asshole they kept telling me He was, did they really think *prayer* was going to work?

I didn't want to go to the Wall. Getting there from my yeshiva meant hiking down the hill, catching a cab to Jerusalem, taking a bus into town, taking a second bus to the very last stop at Jaffa Gate, and then walking a good fifteen minutes through the dark, deserted streets of the Old City. Then there were the Arabs to consider: the cab ride took you through Abu Ghosh, the enormous, usually friendly Arab town on the other side of the mountain, but with the intifada going on, who knew? It was like the riots after the NBA Finals, only in every city, every night, and these guys weren't celebrating. Even if I got to Jerusalem in one unstoned piece, walking through the Old City was no picnic; stories of Arabs stabbing tourists were pretty common, and even if you made it to the Wall alive, there was a pretty good chance you'd be met there by a shower of rock and stone from the Arabs on the Temple Mount above.

I sat up in bed and lit a cigarette.

Then again, what if going to the Wall would help? What if He did read all the notes people put in this wall? What if I went and Baba recovered? What if I didn't go and she died?

I dressed quickly.

—Oh, come on, would He really kill her just because you didn't go to the Wall?

—Well, would He really save her just because I did?

—You're being ridiculous.

—*I'm* being ridiculous?

I grabbed a pen, a small piece of paper, and headed for the Holy of Holies.

I hiked down the hill, caught a cab, took the bus to town, caught the second bus to Jaffa Gate, and walked fifteen minutes through the Old City. I turned down one darkened alleyway after the other, trying to decide how I would begin my note. "God"? Too casual. "Dear God"? Too Judy Blume. "G"? Too Run-DMC. How long did the note have to stay in before God was supposed to answer it? What if it rained overnight and my note got washed away? Did he read them the moment they got shoved into the crack or did it take, like, a day or so? Would taking the note out undo the prayer? What if I begged for mercy, and mercy really meant God's making her die tomorrow? If that was so and I prayed for God to have no mercy—"Hear, O Merciless One"—would she live another few years?

And then, suddenly, there it was; in the dark night sky, beyond a smooth white stone piazza, there it was. Powerful lights illuminated the wall from every direction. It seemed to float, to glow. It was like Times Square, but with God.

I approached the security checkpoint outside the piazza, filled with terror and dread. I didn't want to look at it.

I didn't want to go near it. I didn't want to touch it. My thoughts were filled with God, with creation ex nihilo, with the Bible Codes, with the Holocaust and the Inquisition, with Romans, Hittites, Amorites, and Germans, with Rabbi Akiva being flayed, with the lightness and the void, with sin and redemption, mercy and vengeance.

—*You are* not *King David,* I repeated to myself. —*You are* not *King fucking David.*

—Open, said the *chayelet,* pointing at my jacket.

Her brown skin glistened. Her black Uzi gleamed. As she patted me down, her breasts began a violent uprising of their own, occupied as they were by the restrictive buttons of her IDF blouse.

Good one, God.

The Wailing Wall is 160 feet wide, and stands just over sixty feet tall, and though I once stood at the bottom of the Empire State Building and looked straight up, and though I once stood at the top of the World Trade Center and looked straight down, never before had I felt as insignificant as I did standing at the base of this ancient wall. To my left, an old rabbi with a long silver beard leaned wearily against the wall, his face buried in the crook of his arm. I heard him moaning, and there was resignation in those moans; someone, somewhere, was dying. Nearby, a man knelt down beside his young son and together they slowly reached out to touch the wall. I looked to my right; beside me, a soldier put his hands to the wall, leaned forward and kissed it; he remained there, forehead pressed against the wall, eyes closed, the metal tip of his Uzi scraping lightly against the stone. I reached into my pocket and took out my piece of paper.

Please, I wrote.

I found a small crevice between two large stones at the bottom of the wall, and pressed my note inside.

Behind me, a couple asked another couple if they would take a photo of them.

—Are you getting the Wall in? Make sure you get the Wall.

Then the first couple took a photo of the second couple. A third couple went by and took a photo of the first two couples together.

—That's cute, said the third couple.

—Are you getting in the Wall?

I got on the bus, got on the other bus, jumped in a cab, hiked up the hill, took a few hits of camel shit, and went to sleep.

I phoned New York early the next morning. Baba's fever had subsided. The doctors were cautiously optimistic concerning her condition. I breathed a sigh of relief, and allowed myself to become cautiously optimistic concerning my God. I returned to Jerusalem later that day, and bought myself a new yarmulke. Then I bought a five-volume set of the Five Books of Moses and a book called *The Gates of Repentance.* Afterward I walked to the large open market on Ben Yehuda Street, where God caused me to run into

Naomi, who was there buying pastries for the Sabbath. We sat down at a nearby café and I told her about my grandmother and the Wailing Wall. She smiled to see my new yarmulke. We hardly noticed how late it had become and I walked her to her bus, where I asked her if she was free Saturday night. She said she thought she was, but asked that I phone her later. I said I would, and watched her bus go, and thought, —*Maybe.* I was cautiously optimistic.

I bought a pen at a nearby newsstand, took a bus back into town, a second bus to Jaffa Gate, and hurried through the tight, darkening alleyways of the Old City to the Wailing Wall.

—*Please,* I wrote, and below that, just to avoid confusion: *(Naomi)*

I crushed the paper into a tiny, tight ball. I thought for a moment, unfolded the paper and added a *God:* at the top. Then I signed my name and added a *New York* beneath it, because it sounded a bit imperative without it, the way you'd bark commands at an inferior, and added a *Dear* before the *God,* as I was briefly concerned that my otherwise casual tone might be taken the wrong way. I crammed my note in the wall, got on the bus, got on the other bus, jumped in a cab, hiked up the hill, gave God an hour to do His thing, and phoned Naomi's yeshiva.

—She's in the shower, said the girl who answered the phone. —Getting ready for *Shabbos.*

I tried my best not to think of Naomi in the shower, an act of moral weakness I was sure would void my note. I left a message for her to have a good Sabbath, and asked the girl to let her know I would phone her when it was over, and that I was looking forward to Saturday night.

—Mmm-hmm, said the girl.

I went back to my room filled with love's first gentle stirrings. I ironed my *Shabbos* shirt, smoothed out my new yarmulke, removed the picture of Cindy Crawford, replaced it with a picture of Maimonides, jumped in the shower, and voided my note.

—It'll never happen, said Tzvi during lunch the following day. —She's slumming.

Tzvi knew Naomi from back in New York. Tzvi was religious, too, and, like her, came from a religious Long Island family. Naomi was an FFB, or "*frum* from birth"—an observant person born into an observant family and observant ever since. I was closer to being a BT, or *ba'al teshuva*, "returning in repentance," meaning I had recently become observant after not having been. FFBs never go out with BTs, because BTs and FFBs almost never get married. An FFB's family would never allow it, except in the rare case that the father of the FFB girl had also been a BT, but even then, nobody doubts a BT's commitment like another BT.

—Her father will kill you, said Tzvi, shaking his head as he grabbed another piece of schnitzel. —And then he'll kill her.

I bought *tzitzis*. I began keeping kosher. Kosher food

always made me put on a few pounds, but I believed Naomi to be above such worldly concerns as abs.

Naomi and I would meet in the afternoon and walk together through the streets of Jerusalem; as we were not married, it was forbidden for us to be alone. She would show me houses where famous rabbis had lived, and I would show her where my favorite used-book stores were. She looked concerned.

—But I don't read much of that anymore, I said. —I'm too busy with Torah.

I quit my job at the bar. I began attending morning prayers. Then I began attending evening prayers. Afternoon prayers were still a bit of a pain in the ass.

It was spring now, and the oppressive rains of the Israeli winter were finally giving way to the oppressive heat of summer. One Sunday morning I invited Naomi to join me on an outing to Netanya, but she said that she hadn't been feeling well, and would be spending the day in bed. I tried not to think of her in bed, and went to Netanya alone. I sat on the sandy beach most of the morning until I grew hungry and went off in search of some food. I sat down at a café, ordered a burger, and looked to the café across the way, where I spotted Naomi sitting at an outside table with Tzvi. They were laughing and sharing a milk shake, their beach towels slung casually around their shoulders. They never noticed me. I watched them awhile, paid my check, washed my hands, recited the Grace after Meals, and got the fuck out of there.

Back at the yeshiva, I found a long piece of green toilet

paper pinned to my door. *Mother called,* it read. *Re: Grandmother.*

Specific enough to cause worry now, vague enough for her to be able to deny wanting to have done so later. Classic. I dropped my backpack on my bed and went to the phone.

—What's going on? I asked my mother.

—How are your rabbis? she asked. —Have you been to King David's Tomb?

—How's Baba?

Pause. Sigh. Misery. Death.

—She's back in the hospital. She's weak. She's frail. She's day-to-day.

—Maybe I should go to the Wall, I said. —Have a few words with God.

—That would be nice, said my mother.

I hiked down the mountain, jumped in a cab, got on a bus, got on another bus, and walked fifteen minutes through the narrow alleyways of the Old City. At one point I thought someone had thrown a stone at me, but it was just one I had kicked as I hurried through the narrow alleyways. Darkness had fallen by the time I arrived at the Wall and other than some soldiers and a few old rabbis collecting charity, the Wall was deserted. I pulled out my pen and my crumpled piece of paper. I thought of my grandmother. I thought of my grandfather beside her. I thought of my mother, of Naomi, of Tzvi, and I thought of the new yarmulke on my head and the fat lot of good it had done me. I stood before the wall and flattened the paper against my leg.

Fuck you, I wrote.

I crushed the note into a tiny ball, and jammed it deep into the crevice in front of me, as deep as I could get it to go. I slid the pen back into my pocket, turned, and walked away.

I had gone only about twenty feet before I lost my nerve. Was I crazy? What the hell was I doing? God was going to go fucking bat-shit when He read that. Was I out of my mind?

I rushed back to the Wall and began looking for my note, hoping God hadn't read it yet. I found it and tried desperately to pry the damn thing out with my fingers. It was in there pretty deep, so I tried digging it out with my pen. I had been at it only a few seconds when I was grabbed roughly by my shoulder, spun around, and slammed backward against the wall by a furious Israeli soldier.

—*Asur!* he shouted, grabbing me by the shirt collar. —Prohibited!

—No, no, I said, —you don't understand.

Eight months into my year in Israel and I still couldn't manage more than a stumbling, incoherent mixture of Hebrew and English. The stress of being assaulted by an IDF soldier didn't make me any more articulate.

—*Anee* put, uh, note *bitoch,* inside, *bitoch* Wall . . . *vi'achshav, anee* . . . , uh, *anee* want it back.

—*ASUR!* he shouted again, pointing me away from the wall. —*ASUR!*

I tried arguing, but the Lord had turned the soldier's heart to stone.

—Fine, I said. —Fine. Asshole. *Asshole!*

He took a step toward me and I put my hands up and stepped back.

—Can I write a new one? I asked. —Can I just write a new one?

He pushed me toward the exit.

—I'm not . . . get your goddamn hands . . . listen . . . LISTEN . . . new . . . *chadash* . . . note . . . note *chadash* . . .

He pointed to the bus stop, gave me one last shove, and I slowly walked away, fixing my collar and tucking in my shirt.

—Way to kill my grandmother, you fucking asshole, I called to him, adjusting the yarmulke on my head. —Thanks.

He waved me off. There was nothing left for me to do but go back to my room at the yeshiva and wait for the phone to ring.

—*Baba,* my mother would say. —*She's dead.*

—*No shit, Ma. No fucking shit.*

Baba didn't die that night. She didn't die that month. Maybe God forgot to check his mail. Maybe He wasn't all that bad.

With just two months left before I was to return to New York, my friend's predictions came true. I wigged out.

I bought a black hat and let my sideburns grow long. I spent all day in the study hall. I was moved into the advanced Talmud class, where I was welcomed like a son by the school's most respected scholar.

I was tired of fighting Him. I wasn't getting anywhere and I didn't want to go home. I wrapped myself in the warm security blanket of absolute belief, and it felt good. It felt safe. He controlled the horizontal. He controlled the vertical. Everything, if I just played ball, was going to be all right.

—*I am so thrilled to hear of your amazing progress,* wrote my mother. —*We're so proud of you.*

—*I think I'll stay a second year,* I replied.

Over the next few months and into the following year, I became the most extraordinarily devout Jew for the most extraordinarily ordinary of reasons: I was loved. My rabbis welcomed me into their families. There were rules, of course, but I understood those rules, and when I didn't, there was a rule book I could consult. I ate meals at their dinner tables, came to know their wives and children, and felt for the first time what it was like to be accepted. There was even the suggestion of the hand of Malkie, the head rabbi's chaste and attractive daughter, in marriage. In exchange, all I had to do was wear a yarmulke, and a black hat, and phylacteries, and *tzitzis;* grow a beard and long *peyis;* cut my hair short; study Talmud, the Torah, the Prophets, and the Book of Psalms; keep the Sabbath, and keep kosher, and keep from cursing; and stop reading English books, and stop speaking to my old friends, and stop talking to girls; and promise to move to Jerusalem.

It seemed like a good deal at the time.

15.

*T*he Talmud tells the story of a man named Elisha, one of the most respected scholars of his day. Opinions differ as to how he became a heretic; once he did, though, the Sages would refer to him only as Acher, "the Other." Some say he saw a man violating the rules of Sabbath and not being punished; a moment later, he saw a man obeying the rules of Sabbath (for which the reward was supposed to have been the prolonging of life), whereupon he was bitten by a snake and died.

—Where is the well-being of this man? the Other demanded of God. —Where is the prolonging of his life?

Others say the Other saw the tongue of another scholar lying in the dust after being severed by the Romans.

—The tongue from which pearls of purest ray used to come forth, demanded the Other, —is to lick the dust?

He immediately resolved to commit sin. He violated the Sabbath. He went to a hooker. He went to a hooker and paid her on the Sabbath. He was written out of the Talmud.

Two months into my second year, a truck driven by

Arabs rammed into a van full of students traveling from the yeshiva into Jerusalem. The van had just entered the highway when the truck pulled alongside and the driver of the truck yanked his steering wheel, sending the van tumbling over the guardrail and down a steep cliff on the other side. When word of the accident reached the yeshiva, everyone ran down the hill and watched from a bluff overlooking the highway. A first-year student, here in the Promised Land to reconnect to his God, was the most seriously injured; later we would learn that he was paralyzed from the neck down.

—*Where is the well-being of this man?* I wondered.

The truck full of Arabs had escaped down the highway, and two IDF jeeps had given chase. A few moments later, a roar grew beneath the town of Telshe Stone, and three F-16s appeared as if from nowhere; we would learn later that the town we had been living in for more than a year was built on top of an underground air force base. Nothing here was as it had seemed. *Pictures do not represent actual contents.*

The jets flew in formation overhead. The Americans cheered.

I was confused.

I was distraught.

—I'm confused, I said to Rabbi Wint. —I'm distraught.

—That's the *Suhtun* talking, he said. The evil inclination.

A few weeks later, my grandmother took another turn for the worse. A few weeks after that, my grandfather fell ill. I went to the Wall. I wailed. I crammed dozens of notes into dozens of cracks, but back in New York, dozens of doctors shook their heads and said, —There's not much more we can do.

A month later, walking down a street in the ultra-Orthodox Jerusalem community of Geulah, I caught a glimpse of myself reflected in the storefront window of the men's hat store I frequented. I didn't recognize myself anymore.

—I don't recognize myself anymore, I said to Rabbi Wint.

—That's the *Suhtun* talking, he said.

That night, the *Suhtun* packed my bags and booked me a seat on a Tel Aviv flight to JFK Airport in New York. A week later, I was living in a basement apartment in Queens, a borough of New York City, attending a local yeshiva on Jewel Avenue. I was still wearing my black fedora and *tzitzis* when, a few weeks later, the *Suhtun* bought me a cheeseburger at the McDonald's on Jewel Avenue. Later that night, he drove me into Manhattan and paid a prostitute to service me on Thirty-ninth Street between Ninth and Tenth Avenues.

—I'm Brandi, she said, settling into the passenger seat.

Brandy is made from wine. Wine isn't kosher without a rabbi's certification. The blessing on wine is *hagofen*. Wine needs a blessing even if it's part of a larger meal. If the meal was had by three men or more, it is required to say the extended Grace after Meals. Brandi took off her coat.

—I'm from Minnesota, said Brandi. —Where you from?

—Jerusalem.

—Cool.

When we finished, she got out of the car and closed the door. She had been sitting on my black fedora.

I was confused. I was distraught. I needed a hat block. I put the car in gear and headed home, but only made it a few blocks before I pulled over on the side of Fortieth Street, opened the car door, and vomited.

And was immediately written out of the Talmud.

16.

Our next-door neighbor is named Sharon. Sharon has stage-four cancer. She has other things, too. She has a garden and a dog and a 1996 Jeep Grand Cherokee. She has a husband named Roy—you met him in chapter 1, being run over by a FedEx truck delivering his pornography. Sharon baffles the doctors; she should have died years ago. The doctors are stumped. The doctors are mystified. The doctors can't explain it. The doctors are fools. So is Sharon; Sharon thinks she moved up to Woodstock because she loves nature. She's wrong. She didn't move up here at all; God moved her up here. She's a threat. She's a warning. She's God, increasing His troop presence on my border. Her name isn't Sharon. Her name is Don't Fuck with Me. Her name is This Could Be You. Orli and I often think about moving—farther out, farther away, Europe, Australia, no, maybe New Zealand, away, away, away, the search for a Promised Land continues—but I know we can't. If we move, Sharon dies. Go any further, says God, and the girl gets it. We are, on the morbid, murderous chessboard of the Lord, in check.

Sharon smiles a lot and spends time in her garden. I frown, go to my writing desk, and close the blinds. One of us has cancer, the other has God.

Four weeks before our son was due to be born, I found a lump on Duke's right hind leg. It was the size of a small egg. Orli found another on his left hind leg.

—Swollen lymph nodes, said our vet. —It could be nothing. Or it could be cancer.

He took a sample. He would let us know.

Duke was our Moses. Duke had led us out of Manhattan and into the wilderness of the Hudson Valley. Duke refused to shit. We were spending weekends in the country at the time, where Duke and Harley chased squirrels through the underbrush, sniffed their way through the tall grass, and lay in the hot sun, snapping at flies and mosquitoes. Monday we returned to our cramped apartment in Manhattan; Duke, still just a pup, wouldn't crap until we drove back upstate. Five days. Not a poop. —*I don't shit on concrete,* said Duke. —*I'm sorry, but that's just my policy.*

We were in no position to argue.

The vet looked concerned as he led us out of his office.

—Don't be concerned, he said.

We drove home in silence. We tried not to panic. We got home and took Duke and Harley into the mountains for a hike. It was a clear autumn day, and the leaves were already changing.

—Look at that, said Orli, pointing to a golden maple overhead.

—They're dying.

—Shal.

—No, really. They're beautiful, but they're dying.

—Shal.

—I'm just saying. Tourists are taking snapshots while they're dropping dead. Literally. Dropping dead, right off the tree.

—They've led a good life.

—A short life.

—But happy.

—So what.

I had been making decent progress with my writing lately and figured that was the cause of the threat on Duke's life.

We walked a bit farther, across a dried creek and up a small hill where we sat on a fallen tree and watched Duke and Harley chase chattering chipmunks through the silvery ferns. The motherfuckers were happy he was dying.

The baby began to kick.

—Come on, guys, said Orli. —Let's go home. You'll get 'em tomorrow.

It was mid-October, and I checked the dogs for ticks before letting them back in the house. Afterward, while wiping the mud from Duke's legs, Orli discovered a large cut between the pads of his left paw. We called the vet.

—That's probably it, he said, and explained that an infected cut would cause the lymph nodes to swell. —Come by tomorrow, we'll get him started on a round of antibiotics.

We decided to go out for dinner to celebrate Duke's non-death, and I wondered if this wasn't something all believers might want to do now and then, knowing, after all, Who's running the show: have some friends over, cut some cake, give each other presents and exchange greeting cards. [Cover] I heard He hasn't killed you yet . . . [inside] but the day's not over! Happy Not Dead Day!

I went upstairs, showered, shaved, scratched Duke behind the ears, gave him a treat, turned on my laptop, and dragged the folder labeled "Adventures with the All-Smitey/ALL" into the trash.

In the third grade, Rabbi Kahn told me my name was one of God's seventy-two names, and he forbade me from ever writing it in full. We wrote primarily in Hebrew and Yiddish, so anything on which I wrote my name—God's name—became instantly holy: tests, book reports, *Highlights for Kids*—consequently, they could never be mistreated. It was forbidden to let them touch the floor, it was forbidden to throw them away, it was forbidden to place other papers on top of them.

—Name of the Creator! Rabbi Kahn would shout in horror, pointing at the *McGraw-Hill American History* lying anti-Semitically on top of my Talmud test. —Name of the Creator!

Then I would have to leave the classroom, go upstairs, and walk all the way to the *bais midrash* (study hall), where they kept a brown cardboard box reserved for holy pages without a home: torn prayer books, old Haggadahs, crumbling Talmuds, and the suddenly holy "What I Did This Summer" by God Auslander.

Words have weight. Words have power. Words are holy.

—*Are you sure you want to remove the items in the Trash permanently?* my laptop asked. —*You cannot undo this action.*

I clicked OK.

We went to dinner.

I wanted the steak.

I ordered the fish.

Kosher-ish-er.

17.

On a good week, you might get two or three dead bodies. Then there were weeks where it seemed not a single god-damn person would die.

Impatient, I would phone a man named Motty. Motty was the dispatcher.

—Anything? I would ask.

—Nothing, Motty would say. —Did I beep you?

—No, I would say. —Just checking.

When somebody died, their family would call Motty, and Motty would call me.

—Can you work the weekend? he would ask.

—Yeah, sure. I can work the weekend.

I was a watcher. A *shomer*, in Hebrew. According to Jewish belief, the soul departs the body at the time of death, but sort of hangs out until the body is buried. This can be a terribly distressing time for the soul, what with all the not having a body and the being invisible and the floating around. Therefore, the rabbis decreed, from the moment of death to the moment of burial, the body of the deceased must never be left alone. Traditionally, a member of the deceased's family would sit with the body. But if nobody in the family wanted to sit with a cold dead body in the cold, dark basement of a cold, empty funeral home, the family called Motty. And Motty called me.

—Flushing Meadows Memorial. Jewel Avenue. Schwartz.

—Oceanside Memorial. 21-11 Atlantic Avenue. Finkel.

—Riverdale Hebrew Home. Riverside and 268th Street. Dweck.

The ancient Rabbis tell us that being a watcher is a wonderful mitzvah, or good deed, for which the Almighty Blessed Be He in the World to Come will abundantly reward us. That was all well and good, but Motty paid eighty-five bucks a night—cash—and that was all the reward I needed. I was nineteen years old, back home from Israel, living in a small underground apartment in Kew Gardens, Queens. I had spent my entire life in yeshivas, a monkey in the Ortho-dox Skinner box of God, and though I certainly looked the part with my black pants, white button-down shirt, and black, wide-brimmed fedora, lately I had been feeling less and less Jerusalem and more and more Gomorrah.

—Westside Memorial. Seventh Avenue. Katzenstein.

—Flushing Memorial. Union and 67th. Blumenfeld.

In the beginning, I could count on two jobs a week, three if I was lucky. Friday nights paid double, almost two hundred bucks, but you had to show up Friday evening and stay until after Sabbath ended, late on Saturday night. That was a long time to spend with a dead body, even for me. But two hundred bucks was two hundred bucks, and I was no idiot. I was saving up for a 1982 Ford Mustang convertible.

It was surprisingly pleasant work. The dead were my kind of people.

—Bring a pillow, said Motty the first time he called. —And a *Tehillim. Tehillim* is Hebrew for the Book of Psalms.

—And a snack, he added.

—What kind of snack? I asked.

—Whatever you want, said Motty.

—Like what? Potato chips?

—Potato chips are fine.

—Can I bring a sandwich?

—What kind of sandwich? Motty asked.

—Tuna?

There was a pause while Motty considered the theological implications.

—You can bring a sandwich, Motty decreed.

—Kew Gardens Funeral. Jewel Avenue. Bernstein.

My first job.

Motty told me to be there no later than seven o'clock in the evening, or I wouldn't be able to get in. The security guard would have an envelope for me with eighty-five dollars in it, and he would show me to the body.

I'd never been in a funeral home before. The main floor

was lavishly decorated with Victorian-style furniture, heavy golden drapery, and Italian marble. The guard led me across the lobby to a steel door in the back. We made our way down the bare wooden stairs to the basement, where they kept the bodies, and I remembered the old adage about never looking inside the kitchen of your favorite restaurant.

There was no drapery, and there was no marble. There were a lot of rusty pipes, a noisy boiler, and a dangerously overloaded fuse box. The only furniture, aside from some spare hospital gurneys, was a battered old metal folding chair.

—There you go, said the guard. —There's a toilet at the end of the hall.

—I'm here for Bernstein. Is there a Bernstein here?

He pointed to the large stainless steel door of a commercial refrigerator.

—Bernstein, he said. —I'll be here for another fifteen minutes if you need anything.

I opened my backpack and took out a bottle of purple Gatorade and my book of Psalms. —"Blessed is He, who goes in the path of the righteous . . ." Oh, brother. It seemed a bit late to be giving Bernstein that sort of advice.

—I don't know about you, Bernstein, I said, —but I'm beat.

I lay down on the gurney, put on my Walkman, smoked half a joint, and tried to sleep. I was beginning to wonder if there was such a thing as a soul, but even if there was, I was pretty sure that a glassy-eyed teenage pothead munching his way through a bag of Doritos Cool Ranch tortilla chips wasn't going to offer it a whole heap of consolation.

. . .

Business was good. I enjoyed the independence. I made my own hours. No meetings, no small talk. I was my own boss. It was just me, my sandwich, a small bag of marijuana, a pack of smokes, Guns N' Roses' *Appetite for Destruction,* and some dead guy in a big steel fridge.

Unfortunately, Jewish law stated that a watcher is permitted to watch only one body at a time. If there was only one body in the funeral home, it was clear which body I was watching and there was no need for me to see it. Occasionally, though, the fridge was packed, floor to ceiling, which meant I was required to open the door and make actual eye contact with the body I was meant to be watching. Like most things biblical, this was a less-than-foolproof method that led to a certain amount of confusion. One night, I was told to watch an Epstein. Inside the fridge, I found three of them: a David Epstein, a Gerald Epstein, and a Moshe Epstein.

I caught the funeral director just before he left for the night.

—Yep, he said, we got us a whole load of Epsteins.

We stepped inside the fridge.

—Which Epstein is mine? I asked.

—Which Epstein is mine? he repeated as he checked their tags, as if it were some sort of deep, existential question mankind has pondered since the beginning of time. Which Epstein *is* mine? How will I find my Epstein?

—They give you a first name? he asked.

They hadn't. He suggested I cover my bases and take a

solid look at each of the Epsteins. —Can't go wrong that way, he said.

—Really? I asked. —Are you sure that's kosher?

—It's kosher with me, he said.

I looked at each body in turn. Epstein. Epstein. Epstein.

—OK if I keep this in here? I asked, holding up my bottle of purple Gatorade.

—It's kosher with me, he said.

A ghoulish economics developed. All that dying was making me a nice living. One dead paid my Amex bill. Three deads covered my share of the rent. A weekend job covered me for weed and food, and soon I was done for the month; every dead after that was just gravy. Two deads got me some new Air Jordans. Three deads was a new TV. If Motty could have guaranteed me a solid extra dead a week, I would have ordered HBO. But I was no fool. I was saving up for a 1982 Ford Mustang convertible.

Death didn't bother me. I'd never personally known anybody who died, but after nineteen years in Orthodox yeshivas, I was pretty familiar with death.

The Jewish holidays all seem to involve someone killing us, someone trying to kill us, or our praying to God so that He doesn't kill us Himself. Jewish history was the same: if the Babylonians weren't trying to kill us, it was the Romans. If it wasn't the Romans, it was the Spanish. And if it wasn't the Spanish, it was the Germans. Every Holocaust Remembrance Day, we were led into the school auditorium to watch hours and hours of newsreel footage so graphic that we needed special permission forms signed by our parents. This was never a problem for me. My mother lived for death. Nothing made her happier than sadness. Nothing made her more joyful than melancholy. She worked as a medical assistant for a local pediatrician, and the tragedies she witnessed there were at least as much a perk as the dental coverage.

—Boy came into the office today, she would say at dinner. —Hepatitis. She would pause to take a long, slow sip of her soup. —C, she would add.

My father would pound the table with his fist.

—Do we have to listen to this crap every goddamn meal? he would bark, taking his plate into the kitchen to finish eating.

Indeed we did.

—It's a death sentence, she would say once he'd left. —Kid doesn't have a chance.

Lung infections. Genetic disease. Spinal meningitis. I ate as quickly as I could, hoping to get through dessert before the gastrointestinal disorders.

Perhaps this was also Jeffie's fault. Perhaps my mother hadn't been as fixated on death before he came—and left—but it was a tragedy from which she refused to recover. Between Jeffie and my relatives who died in the Holocaust, my mother had more pictures of the dead on our walls than she had of the living, and the dead seemed to be having a better time: my brother hated my mother and resented me; my mother loathed my brother and doted on me and my sister; my sister hated my brother and defended my mother; I envied my brother and pitied my mother; my father hated us all; and my mother sighed, washed the dishes, and sang mournful Yiddish songs about the miserable futility of life. All of this, the family story goes, because Jeffie died.

Between my mother and my rabbis, death wasn't the worst thing I could imagine. In fact, by the time I was nineteen, I couldn't care less about it.

A few months after I started, Motty hired a second watcher. Business was good. Motty was branching out. He was expanding to meet customer demand. And I didn't like it.

The new watcher's name was David. David was Motty's cousin, and I was convinced he was receiving preferential treatment. He was given nearly every weekend job—the two-hundred-dollar types—and I was pretty sure he was getting first pick of the midweek gigs as well.

Impatient, I would phone Motty.

—Anything? I would ask.

—Nothing, Motty would say. —Did I beep you?

—No. Just checking.

—I'll beep you.

The third watcher Motty hired was named Shmuel. Shmuel was an ultra-Orthodox yeshiva student who knew Motty from synagogue and cynically pretended that the money didn't matter to him. —I need the mitzvahs! he would say to Motty, clapping his hands with righteous glee. Pretty soon I was down to one lousy dead every two or three weeks.

Impatient, I phoned Motty.

—Anything? I asked.

—Nothing, Motty said. —Did I beep you?

—Nothing? I asked. —Nobody's died in the past three weeks in all of Brooklyn and Queens?

—Blessed is He who heals the sick, said Motty.

—Oh, bullshit, I said, and slammed down the phone. Even death was about who you knew. Motty never beeped me again.

I had almost a whole month off from death—no funeral homes, no refrigerators, no suffering of any kind—when my mother called to tell me that my grandmother had passed away.

—She's at the Zion Gate Memorial Home, she said, —you know where that is?

My mother had been proud of my watching career, and had been sad to hear of its sudden demise. She was like a Yankee fan who knew someone who worked for the team; she'd known someone on the inside of sorrow, her favorite sport.

—I know where it is, I said.

She blew her nose into the phone and sighed deeply.

—So unexpected, she said. —That's the hardest part.

My grandmother died from Alzheimer's, a disease she'd had for well over seven years.

I got to Zion Gate, walked heavily down the stairs, threw my bag on a nearby gurney, and dropped into my old seat on the metal folding chair beside the fridge.

I didn't know my grandmother well—the disease had killed her mind years before it finally came back for her body—but I had some war memories of her from my childhood, memories I desperately ran through my mind, trying for once to feel something, anything, for the dead body inside that fridge. I remembered how when I was young, she would bring us Rice Krispies Treats that she made with real Fluff, which everyone knows isn't kosher.

—Don't tell your mother, she'd whisper.

But it was no use. I sat there fuming, picturing my mother upstairs, the belle of the misery ball. She would be sighing and hugging and reciting Yiddish aphorisms about the inescapable brutality of our wretched lives.

I felt like Al Pacino in that Mafia movie—"Just when I thought that I was out, they pull me back in."

I opened my Gatorade, took a few hits off a joint, put on my Walkman, and tried to get some sleep. It was already eleven p.m., and I had to be at my new job at the hardware store early the next morning.

Let the rest of them mourn.

I was saving up for a 1982 Ford Mustang convertible.

18.

I was twenty years old and having a difficult time meeting women. My forefather Isaac, I imagined, must have had a difficult time meeting women, too. After the abusive childhood he suffered at the hands of his Godoholic father, who could relate to him? Who could understand what he had been through? And who would accept the overbearing Lord who accompanied him wherever he went? I imagined him suffering, as I was, a succession of awkward, shallow relationships with people who would never understand who he was, and if they did, would never want to be with him.

There was the religious girl from Long Island who encouraged me to be more religious. When I did become more religious, she decided she liked me better less religious.

There was the penis-phobic blond-haired adoptee, who enjoyed encouraging me through unfulfilled sexual promises to become less religious. Having become less religious, she decided she wanted someone more religious.

My only friends were the religious ones I had made while in Israel, friends who would never speak to me if they knew what I was really thinking. Or occasionally eating. I was as lonely and distraught as I had ever been in my life. And then the phone rang.

—What are you doing tomorrow night? Leah asked.

Leah's father was a rabbi. Her uncles on her father's side were rabbis, and her mother's brothers were also rabbis. Leah was forever doing mitzvahs, or good deeds. She visited the sick. She raised charity for the poor. She volunteered at the local synagogue. She was trying to keep me religious. Saturday nights, Leah would phone me and excitedly tell me Torah lessons she'd heard from her father that *Shabbos*.

—Do you know what Reb Zalman wrote about the importance of charity? she would ask. —Have you ever seen the Rambam's lecture on penance? —Have you read Rav Moshe's answer on why smoking is prohibited according to the Ten Commandments?

—No, I would say, lighting a cigarette away from the phone. —Have you ever read Samuel Beckett?

—No, she would say. —What did he write?

—That life is a pointless, tragicomic cycle of sorrow and isolation punctuated by desperate moments of ludicrous belief in a savior that never arrives.

—Are you smoking? asked Leah.

—No, I would lie.

Then, more Reb Zalman.

—So? she asked, —what are you doing tomorrow night?

I told her I was free, and she asked if I could help her friend move into a new apartment. Her friend's name was

Orli, and she had just come over from London. Orli was another one of Leah's Jew-saving projects and she wanted us to meet. Two drowning people, she hoped, would together learn to swim. We did, in fact, but not in the direction she had hoped.

The following evening, I sat in my car outside the address Leah had given me, waiting for her and Orli to arrive. There was a knock on my window.

—Shalom? asked Orli.

—Yes?

—Bloody hell, she said laughing. —You had me frightened half to death.

She was beautiful—green eyes and long, dark hair, with the accent of the queen of England and the mouth of Sid Vicious. It made me all Benny Hill.

—What are you reading? she asked, pointing at the book on the passenger seat.

—*Crime and Punishment,* I said.

—Is it good?

—It's funny, I said.

—What's it about?

—It's about a guy who murders an old lady.

—And?

—And he worries about it for three hundred pages.

—That does sound funny.

It was Isaac's lucky night.

After all of Orli's boxes had been moved upstairs, Leah went home, and Orli and I talked. We talked and talked and talked, and we didn't stop talking until the sun came up the next morning. We talked over breakfast, talked over lunch, talked as we walked around Central Park, talked over dinner, and talked straight through the night again to the following morning. Orli had been through her own personal traumas, and though different in kind from mine, they were similar enough in effect. The odds were astounding.

—*Well,* said Isaac, —*my father, he, uh, sort of . . . well, he tried to sacrifice me to his God.*

—*Get OUT!* said the woman beside him at the bar, giving him a playful nudge. —*Mine, too!*

This was the closest I'd ever come to finding someone who might love and accept me for who I was, and I wasn't about to risk it by doing something stupid like revealing myself completely. There were just some things she would never understand—the God, the sexual obsession, the guilt, the shame. Over breakfasts of Earl Grey tea and Walker's shortbread cookies (*traif!*), I gazed into her green-flecked eyes and knew I would love her, and lie to her, for the rest of my life.

My mother phoned.

—Is she Jewish? she asked.

—Yes, I said.

—Jewish from London?

I hung up. Jews in Monsey have a hard time imagining there are Jews anywhere else in the world, and if there are— if—they are certainly less devout. My mother phoned a rabbi in Monsey, who phoned a rabbi in Manhattan, who phoned a rabbi in central London, who phoned a rabbi in North Finchley.

—I hear she comes from a good family, my mother reported.

I hung up.

—You've been certified kosher, I said to Orli.

—*Mazel tov,* she said. Then she made a joke about her being safe to eat, and I nearly fainted.

I was trying not to get too optimistic. I didn't know what God was up to, but I was pretty sure He was only setting me up for heartbreak. She probably had a husband. She probably had an inoperable brain tumor. She probably had a penis. We went to a New York Rangers game a few weeks later, where for three long periods she shouted *Wanker!* at the referee while I, having fallen in love, waited for a puck to ricochet off the goal post, sail into the stands, and strike her, hard, on the invisible X the Almighty had drawn between my beloved's eyes. That would be so God.

But Orli made it out of the Garden alive (—Close game, she had said afterward. —Yeah, I said, —very close . . .), and I took that as an all-clear from God. Six months later, we were married and living in the East Village.

Once you start burning pornography, it's almost impossible to stop. I had been penitently burning porn magazines ever since the sixth grade, but as a fourteen-year-old in a yeshiva high school located 139 short blocks away from Times Square, my burn rate increased dramatically.

God's appetite for testing me was as insatiable as my lust for failing, and his plans were often staggeringly complex. On May 25, 1961, for instance, He caused Steven Hirsch to be born in Cleveland, Ohio. One year later, in 1962, a girl named Ginger Allen is born in Rockford, Illinois, and four years later, in 1966, Melissa Bardizbanian is born in Pasadena, California. A decade later, in 1977, Steven's parents move to the San Fernando Valley, just outside Los Angeles, where his father starts an adult video company. Four years later, God causes Ginger Allen's grandfather to take ill, and she visits him in California, where she decides to remain. Ginger answers an ad for figure models, and quickly receives an offer to pose for *Penthouse* magazine. It is now 1983. Over in Pasadena, Melissa Bardizbanian is running away from home, and down in the San Fernando Valley, Steven Hirsch is selling adult videos for a company called CalVista, where God causes him to meet a man named David James. One year later, in 1984, Steven and David found a company called Vivid Video, and they sign Ginger Allen—now Ginger Lynn—to an exclusive contract. Melissa changes her name to Christy Canyon, I begin high school at an uptown Manhattan yeshiva, and Christy and Ginger make a film for Vivid called *The Night of Loving Dangerously.* I take the A train down to Times Square, wait for pedestrian traffic to thin out a bit, duck into Peepland on Forty-second between Broadway and Sixth Avenue, and discover the video on the shelf labeled New Releases, which are always discounted by thirty percent. I pick it up, I put it down. I leave, I return. Up above, God scoots up to the edge of His seat and peers down, elbows on His knees, remote control in hand, thumb resting lightly on KILL.

Soon I had a lot more to burn than just magazines. I burned books, videotapes, and sex toys, and the soiled T-shirts whose ruin they had caused. I burned plastic, rubber, and latex. I burned vaginas, mouths, and asses. Not all of them burned easily; silicone had to be buried. The Doc Johnson Vanessa Del Rio Vibrating Sex Mouth took half a can of lighter fluid to ignite, but finally it did, blackening like my soul, the smoke rising up to heaven as Vanessa's red lips softened and twisted into a pained, hellish grimace that melted at last into a dark brown puddle of non-titillating plastic. All that remained of my sin was the small metallic vibrator, sitting shamefully on the ground, bringing nobody to the frenzied heights of anything.

And then one day, when I was sixteen, I went upstairs.

The sign read "Live Nude Girls," and though I'd seen it before, and heard them up there, too—calling, shouting, laughing—it sounded to me like the bowels of hell, or maybe the uterus; I imagined the porno store to be something like an M. C. Escher drawing, where stairs that appear to be going up are actually going down, except Escher's stairs didn't have pink neon lights in the treads, and they didn't have silhouettes of naked women on the risers, and there wasn't a tall woman at the top—or bottom?—lifting her bikini top to flash me her tits.

I climbed slowly up (or down?), locked myself in the first

empty booth I could find, and welcomed the darkness that surrounded me. I turned to find myself facing a two-foot-tall, one-foot-wide window blocked by a wooden blind. I deposited some quarters into the illuminated slot beneath it, and the blind lifted. (I briefly considered an outdoor art project, in which these token slots would be placed randomly on walls around the city. My thesis? Men will put a quarter into any slot, anywhere, without question, to see what is on the other side; I knew I would.) The window looked out onto a raised circular stage; next to me I could see other windows, with other men looking out, the stage raised to such a height that our faces, full of sadness and desperation, were only a foot or so above the floor of the stage. A small group of black and Hispanic women, naked except for their shoes and Kool 100s, stood smoking and chatting until a window rose up; then they scrambled madly to be the first one in front of it, not always extinguishing their cigarettes beforehand, squatting ungracefully before the windows, the first live naked women I had ever seen.

—*What was God waiting for?* I wondered.

A naked woman squatted down before my window and shouted.

—Excuse me? I said.

—Two for tits, she shouted, —three for pussy.

I had no idea what she was talking about. She extended her arm through the window and held her hand open.

—Two for tits, baby. Three for pussy.

I reached into my pocket. All I had was my yarmulke and a five.

Five bucks and thirty seconds later, a line had been crossed. I was weak. I was shameful. I was a failure. I was no greater than the lowest animal on Earth. I had no control over my desires. I had placed my body before my soul. I had chosen this world over the next. I had eaten from the tree of knowledge. I had denied my essential goodness. I had extinguished the flame of Jewishness within my soul. I had turned my back on God. I had murdered a million Jewish souls. I had behaved in the manner of the nations of the world. I had defiled the body God had lent me, His fury certain to be as fearsome as His vengeance. The window slid shut, and the darkness that surrounded me now filled me completely. I thought He might kill me right there, in the booth in the theater in the center of the city I never should have entered. I imagined the scene as my dead body (stabbed by a stripper? shot by a pervert? heart attack in a buddy booth?) was carried out of the store, my mother, the first on the scene, wailing —*But why???* as the people on the sidewalk gathered to watch, saddened, sure, but understanding, along with Mom, that, well, I had it coming.

Burning would no longer suffice. Burning was too easy. My sin had been too great. I wasn't fooling Anybody with this pyro-penance crap.

That night, after showering and saying good night to my mother, I went to my bedroom, stood naked in front of my desk, and dropped the heaviest dictionary I could find onto my tool of the evil inclination.

Merriam-Webster.

Hardcover.

Unabridged.

A new era had begun.

—Goddamnit, my father would shout from the garage. —Where the hell's all my C-clamps gone?

Fire had been replaced with anguish, burning with punishing, lighter fluid with hand tools. Jews don't have a tradition of self-flagellation, but we beat ourselves on the chest every Day of Atonement, and I had studied the Talmud's intricate discussions concerning the various forms of capital punishment—stoning, burning, beheading, and strangulation:

> *This is the implementation of the commandment of burning: We insert him in manure up to his knees, we put a hard garment inside a soft garment and wrap them around his neck. The witnesses pull in both directions, making his mouth open. One lights a wick and throws it into his mouth, burning his innards.*
>
> *Rabbi Yehuda asks: If they strangle him, will the mitzvah of burning not be fulfilled? The Talmud reassures him: We use tongs to force his mouth open. What is a wick? the Talmud asks. Hot lead, someone answers.*

This continues for some time.

My mother couldn't understand where all her cooking utensils were going.

—Did somebody take my meat tenderizer? How the hell am I supposed to make the brisket without my meat tenderizer?

On the plus side, we weren't going through matches like we used to.

· · ·

In chapter 1 of the Chapters of the Fathers, the Sages instruct each and every Jew to build a fence around the Torah—to create laws and prohibitions and protections that will safeguard him from temptation and sin. At twenty-one years of age, I hoped that marriage would be my fence against the temptation of sex and pornography, but it was soon obvious that I was going to need more than just a fence: more like a rampart, something with a moat and a bunch of crocodiles. Six months into my marriage and there was already a *Black Tail* magazine under my mattress and a *Barely Legal* stuffed behind the bookshelf.

One night, as Orli slept soundly beside me, I gently lifted the remote from her hand, lowered the volume on the television, and switched from *Cheers* to *The Robin Byrd Show.* Afterward, I punished myself. For being weak. For being a sinner. For failing my wife, for failing myself, for becoming my father. For incurring the wrath of God, wrath that no longer affected me, but affected Orli, affected our marriage. It was a night of particularly severe self-reproach. I awoke the following morning in agony.

—Something's wrong, I said to Orli.

—What is it?

—Something.

An hour later, I waddled into the emergency room of the New York Hospital on East Sixty-eighth Street.

—Testicular torsion, said the doctor.

—Never heard of them, I grimaced.

—It's not a band, he said. —It's a very serious medical condition; we need to operate immediately.

He explained that I had "dislodged" one of my testicles, constricting the spermatic cord, cutting off the blood flow, and necessitating emergency surgery. I hoped God was enjoying this as much as I expected He was.

—Will you consent to the surgery? asked the doctor.

I pressed my fingertips against my eyes and shook my head in disbelief.

—You had me at "dislodged," I answered.

The nurse offered to phone Orli, and handed me a legal form authorizing the hospital to remove my testicles.

—*Okey-dokey,* I said to God as they wheeled me into the operating room. —*I think this makes us even.*

I awoke sometime later in my hospital bed, fortunate to find my testicles exactly where I had left them. I was unfortunate, however, in that the New York Hospital is a teaching hospital. Once every morning and again every night, the surgeon would come by with a group of young medical students, throw off my bedcovers, point to my swollen testicles, and ask, —Now, who can tell me what we have here?

The male students covered their crotches and looked away; the female students—blond and beautiful, every one—covered their mouths, puffed out their cheeks, and leaned in for a closer view.

Oh, yes—He was enjoying this very, very much.

19.

*A*nd Abraham arose, and he went forth.

And, behold, he was disappointed.

The first year of our marriage was difficult. I hated my family but spoke to them kindly, loved my wife but spoke to her curtly. The East Village wasn't working out. This was supposed to have been my un–Promised Land, the final chapter in the reverse Exodus my life had become—I had fled the land of my forefathers, the land of Abraham, Isaac, and Jacob, and Rabbi Kahn and Rabbi Blowfeld, the land of yeshivas and Yahweh and violent rabbis and the religiously conditional love of my family, and had made my way to Manhattan, the land of freedom and anonymity, of foreign films and incomprehensible plays and all nude girls, to the place that Woody Allen had shown me. Instead I got Martin Scorsese.

Good one, God.

We had rented an adorable ground-floor studio on East Thirteenth Street, across the way from the cutest little soup kitchen, and just down the road from a to-die-for outpatient methadone clinic. At night we fell asleep to the ungentle sounds of homeless people going through the trash just outside our window, of our landlord shouting at them, and of glass bottles shattering as he threw them out his window to chase them off. Soon we drifted off to sleep, as outside our window, heroin addicts and mental patients quietly collected the largest, sharpest pieces of jagged glass from the front stoop.

—Good night, honey, said Orli.

—Good night, love, I said.

—Gonna cut that faggot son of a bitch come morning, said the heroin addict.

I held my middle finger up at God. Orli looked at me and brushed my cheek with her hand. I expected my relationship with God to worry her, but in fact, it had only made her sad.

I tried to look at the bright side. Yes, there was a man taking a shit on the front stoop. But I was close to work. Pot dealers delivered. And I wasn't in Monsey.

—It's not so bad, I said, passing the joint to Orli. —We can make it work.

We struggled. Manhattan was cold, dead, and full of psychotics—psychotics dressed in garbage bags who lived out of shopping carts; psychotics in sharp suits and ties who worked twenty hours a day at jobs they despised; psychotics who walked around as if on film, posing and preening as if surrounded by imaginary paparazzi and film crews. I preferred the homeless man berating his imaginary mother; at least I could understand the impulse. Instead of atheism,

I found polytheism; there were more gods here than there had been in Monsey—not as vengeful, perhaps, but inspiring no less devotion among their worshippers: the upper gods—fashion, money, success, power—and the lower gods— car, health club membership, address (there was a holy war brewing, I was sure, between the Below Fourteenth Streetians and the Above Fourteenth Streetians). There was a bible called *The New York Times,* one called *The Village Voice,* a god named Frank Rich. Behold, here was "Trump, Lord of Money," and in the East Village, where we lived, a temple called Kim's Video, staffed by the surly, underweight, illcomplected acolytes of a god named Sergei Eisenstein, creator of montage, resurrector of editing, who had brought forth unto the world *Potemkin,* and delivered unto His people proto-didactic filmic symbolism.

Only the nouns had changed.

God damn you, Woody Allen.

A few weeks later, the building next door to ours appeared on the cover of the *New York Post.* This was the headline:

CRACKHOUSE.

And Abraham packed up his shit, and he moved to the Upper East Side.

We rented a decrepit railroad apartment in a collapsing building on Second Avenue and Seventy-first Street. The floor sloped along its entire length at a fifteen-degree angle, a poorly written metaphor for the emotional health of its tenants.

—Good one, I said to God. —I get it . . . *tilted*. Hack.

Around the time of our first wedding anniversary, I quit my job writing advertising copy in order to write something else, but six months later, I was no closer to figuring out what that something else might be. I'd had only a couple of ideas that I'd felt like pursuing. One was to masturbate. The other was to smoke pot. Lately I'd been working on a third idea, sort of a pastiche of the first two. I'd expected to earn some money freelancing in the advertising business, but God thought it would be funny to cause an industry-wide recession the week after I quit. I slept all day and stared at blank pages all night. I had a favorite *Robin Byrd* episode. I read Kafka, Gogol, Dostoyevsky. I felt like Beckett looked. I agreed to see a psychiatrist.

I told Dr. Hirsch that I had been thinking a lot about suicide.

—Not about committing it, I said. —Just about its theological implications.

It seemed, I explained, to be the only real free choice we had. Surely it must the Achilles' heel of God's whole little creation project, a project conceived in narcissism and dominance, a project whose cardinal rule taking your own life flagrantly violated: *You'll stay in your room until I sayeth you can come out.* The fact He deemed it a sin only lent further credence to my theory: He was a control freak and it probably drove Him crazy that a man could take his own life—that all of mankind could, en masse, end His whole miserable creation—and that maybe that was reason enough to do it, because fuck Him, because this might be His sandbox and He might be able to punish me whenever He wanted. But guess what, O Lord? Guess what, There Shall Be No Other God but Me? Guess what, Love Me and Fear Me, guess what? I can take my shovel and go home anytime I want.

—Do you really think God is punishing you? asked Dr. Hirsch.

His naïveté astounded me.

—I don't *think* He is. I *know* He is.

He asked me to call him Ike. I told Ike that I felt like the biblical Egyptians, plagued by God with a darkness that never lifted. He told me his fee was $350.

—A week?

—A session. But we need to see each other twice a week.

That I couldn't afford sanity drove me mad, but my choices were simple: stay crazy, move out of Manhattan, or return to work. Fortunately, the head of the agency I'd recently left had assured me I could come back anytime. His name was Nick.

—We're family here, Nick had said.

I went to see him after my first visit with Ike.

—Can I come back? I asked.

—No, said Nick.

Orli and I moved out of Manhattan four weeks later. After the punishing expense of Manhattan, we'd decided suburban life was worth another try. We had been married for only a year and a half, and, not counting Monsey and London, we were already 0 for 3 on Promised Lands.

Teaneck, New Jersey, is a quiet upper-middle-class community with large Tudor homes, well-kept lawns, and shady streets, assuming you aren't black. If you're black, Teaneck is a run-down lower-class community with a couple of strip malls, a video rental shop, and a Popeye's Chicken. Fifty years ago, Teaneck was selected from over ten thousand towns as America's model community, a place where people lived together in tree-lined, sun-dappled racial harmony. But today, the Jews don't often venture into the black area, which begins at Teaneck Road, and the blacks don't often venture into the Jewish area, which begins at Queen Anne Road. The two-block-long area between Teaneck Road and Queen Anne Road is therefore a sort of suburban American green zone. It has a Walgreens, a Chinese laundry, a heavy twenty-four-hour police presence, and an apartment complex called Terrace Circle.

The Terrace Circle complex, a dozen identical squat brick buildings set in an uneven circle around a small grassy courtyard, is tenanted almost exclusively by young Jewish newlyweds who dream of the day they will move across Queen Anne Road to a four-bedroom, two-and-a-half-bath-Tudor Promised Land of their own. They see themselves not unlike the settlers in the West Bank of Israel, daring to live in such close proximity to their enemies in order to fulfill their destiny; only here, the Arabs were African Americans, Gaza was Teaneck, the settlements were two-bedroom garden apartments with on-site laundry, and the Promised Land was a thirty-year mortgage on a two-and-a-half-bath with a cook's kitchen and two-car garage on the Queen Anne Road side of town.

The day Orli and I moved into apartment 3B, 1492 West Terrace Circle, my sister-in-law drove us around for a quick tour of the neighborhood. She and my brother had sojourned in Terrace Circle for many years, and had moved only recently. Their new house, on the proper side of Queen Anne, was a multilevel, multi-bedroom, multibath, with a swing set out back and two cars out front. Tudor.

—There's the kosher butcher, she said. —And there's the Dunkin' Donuts. Dunkin' Donuts is kosher, but not the tuna fish, or the eggs. Not sure about the crullers. That's Rabbi Hecht's synagogue. Very Orthodox. You know Rabbi Mandelbaum? There's his synagogue. Our synagogue is up this way . . .

I stared glumly out the minivan window as we drove past the houses and the synagogues and the yeshivas and the houses and the synagogues and yeshivas. The night before I had gone to sleep in a Lee Friedlander photograph; this morning I had woken up in one by Roman Vishniac.

—Did I show you the kosher pizza store? asked my sister-in-law.

—Wow, I said, indicating my wristwatch. —Cable guy.

It was Friday, May 6, 1994: game four of the Stanley Cup Conference semifinals between the Rangers and the

Washington Capitals was scheduled for the following Sabbath afternoon.

The cable guy left, and I closed the door behind him. They say you can never go home again, but I seemed to be having the opposite problem; I felt as if, under cover of night, I'd daringly escaped from Auschwitz, gotten past the guards, evaded the dogs, run for the woods, and clambered onto a passing train that two hours later pulled straight into Treblinka.

I leaned against the door, looked up at the ceiling, scowled, and gave God the finger.

—Fuck you, I said.

The telephone rang. The machine picked up. It was my mother. She congratulated us on our move with a string of Yiddish expressions, and said how wonderful it was that we were only thirty minutes away. Then more Yiddish.

—No, said the Lord. —Fuck you.

There are thirty-nine categories of work that are prohibited on the Sabbath. Category 37, kindling a fire, also rules out the use of anything electrical, including a television. I had decided to switch on the television Friday afternoon—before Sabbath began—and just leave it on until Sabbath ended, twenty-five hours later on Saturday night. This wasn't, technically, "being in the spirit of Sabbath," but failing to be in the spirit of Sabbath wasn't technically a sin, and the Rangers were very likely nine victories away from winning the Stanley Cup finals for the first time in fifty-four years. I switched on the television, turned down the volume, and draped a washed-out bath towel over the screen to hide the flickering blue light of our moral weakness from the neighbors.

—Do you really think that if you turn on the TV on Sabbath, God will make the Rangers lose? asked Orli.

Her naïveté astounded me.

—I don't *think* He will. I *know* He will.

Orli put her arm around me. —They really did a number on you, she said.

We showered, dressed, lit the Sabbath candles, and walked to my brother's house for the Friday-night Sabbath meal. He showed us his house. He showed us his yard. He showed us his new sedan. He showed us his new fishing rods.

—Did you see my new TV? he asked.

—We better get going, said Orli. I apologized for her, feigned resistance, and we hurried home together, arm in arm, through the darkening night.

The following morning, I trudged into the living room and stared out the window in horror: dozens of young married couples in expensive suits and even more expensive dresses, at least half of the women cradling babies, were standing around on the patchy lawn at the heart of the Terrace Circle complex playing show-and-tell with their neckties, hats, and newborns (sitting on the lawn was prohibited because the grass could dye your clothes—dyeing, category 15. Some held that it was also a violation of plowing, category 2, and, should the grass be pulled out of the ground by the heel of your shoe, reaping, category 3). The window was open, and I could hear the couples with babies telling the couples without babies how great it was to have babies. The couples without babies were saying, —We can't wait.

—*Im yirtzeh Hashem* by you, the couples with babies replied. *If God so desires it, by you.*

Orli and I decided to go for a walk.

—Do I have to wear Sabbath clothes? I asked.

—How should I know? asked Orli.

—What are you wearing?

—I'm wearing clothes.

—Those are Sabbath clothes.

—A skirt is Sabbath clothes?

—Yes, I said.

—You just don't like skirts.

—Because people wear them on Sabbath.

—Because you think they make me look Jewish.

—They do make you look Jewish. They make you look like you're Jewish and it's Sabbath.

—Just tell me, Shal, she said. —I don't know these people. Can I wear this or not?

—I don't know.

—What about these trainers?

—What about them?

—Can I wear them? Will the Rangers lose if I wear trainers on Sabbath?

I considered the question.

—Probably.

—Fine. She shrugged. —Then I'll wear shoes. I don't mind.

I knew it. I knew we had to wear Sabbath clothes.

We walked across the lawn, down the Terrace Circle driveway and headed away from the complex.

—*Gut Shabbos,* someone called to us.

—*Gut Shabbos,* we called back.

—*Gut Shabbos,* called someone else.

—*Gut Shabbos,* we called back.

—*Gut Shabbos,* called a third someone.

—Piss off, I muttered.

Finally we crossed State Street and found a small playground, where we sat on some swings and smoked a joint (category 37, kindling a fire). The Sages say that one may violate the Sabbath only in order to save a Jewish life, but as my new antidepressants had yet to kick in, I figured God would give me a pass on a couple of Sabbath-morning hits.

—It's not so bad, I said, passing the joint to Orli. —We can make it work.

She took a hit, stared down at her Sabbath shoes, and nodded.

It was past two o'clock in the afternoon when we finally returned to Terrace Circle, and we were pretty seriously high (category 11, baking). People were just finishing their Sabbath lunches and stumbling outside, the men patting their distended bellies with pride, the women doing the same with their babies.

—Which synagogue will you guys be going to? asked Daniel Something.

—The one, you know, I said. Rabbi . . .

—Hecht? he offered.

—Yup, I said.

—Hecht, said Orli.

—I hate that synagogue, said Daniel's wife. —You should go to Rabbi Levine's synagogue. The people are much cooler.

—Rabbi Levine's synagogue? Her husband took offense. —What's so great about Rabbi Levine's synagogue?

—Nothing, said Daniel's wife. The baby she was holding began to cry. —I just think they'd like it better.

—So they wouldn't like Rabbi Hecht's synagogue? asked Daniel. —How do you know what synagogue they would like? Do you know who Rabbi Hecht studied with? Rabbi Soloveitchik!

—So? shouted his wife. The baby was screaming.

—So? Daniel shouted back. —So?

—*Im yirtzeh Hashem* by you, I said, which caused Orli to collapse on the lawn in a fit of laughter.

—*Yirtzeh!* she shouted, laughing hysterically and rolling on the lawn, dyeing (category 15), plowing (category 2), and reaping (category 3) with reckless pot-headed abandon.

By the time we returned to our apartment, the Rangers game was half over. We closed the blinds, locked the front door, froze in place for a moment when neighbors on their way out stopped at our apartment door to listen, then lifted the towel off the TV screen, pulled on our Rangers jerseys (mine home, hers away), and sat side by side on the couch, biting our nails and trying not to shout at every slap shot or scream at every penalty. The score was tied at two goals apiece.

—So do we have to invite them over now? I asked.

—Who?

—The Whoevers. Daniel and his wife.

—I don't know, said Orli.

—I think we do, I said.

—We don't have to do anything.

The Rangers wasted a power-play opportunity and turned the puck over twice in their own zone.

—I think we have to invite them over, I said.

Thirty minutes later, the final buzzer sounded and the Rangers had lost, 4–2. I cursed the refs, I cursed the Capitals, and I cursed myself for leaving the television on in the first place. I looked up and scowled at the heavens.

The Rangers won game five, eliminating the Capitals and moving on to face the New Jersey Devils in the best-of-seven conference finals the following week. I checked the calendar for any theological conflicts: game four was scheduled for a Saturday afternoon, and game seven, if there was one, was scheduled for the following Friday night. I made a deal with God that if the Rangers won the first three games, I would leave the TV off for game four. On the other hand, if the Devils won the first three games, I would also leave the TV off: at worst I'd miss watching the Rangers getting eliminated from the playoffs.

There would be no negotiation concerning game seven.

By the end of the week, the Rangers led the series 2–1. I watched Saturday's game, which the Devils won 3–1. Monday night's game was even worse: Devils, 4–1. I sat back on my couch and stared at the television in disbelief as the Rangers skated, heads lowered, off the ice. They were one game away from elimination. This is the kind of God I was dealing with, the kind who leads Moses all the way through the desert, right to the edge of the Promised Land, and doesn't let him in—kills him, in fact—because he once, years ago, hit a rock. A *rock*. And now this. He waits fifty-four years. He brings Messier over from Canada. He brings Gorbachev to power in order to institute *glasnost* so that Kovalev can come to New York and give the Rangers some much-needed firepower in the right-wing position. And now—*now*—He was going to toss them out of the playoffs.

—We shouldn't have watched those games, I said.

—What games? asked Orli.

—The ones on Sabbath.

Orli sat down beside me and patted my thigh.

—Hey, she said, her voice soft. —Come on.

Wednesday night, God let the Rangers win game six, in order to set up a game seven showdown on a Friday night. Such a drama queen.

Friday afternoon I saw Ike. I wanted to talk about God. He wanted to talk about my family. An advertising agency

in midtown had offered me a long-term freelance assign-
ment, and though I loathed myself for taking it, I loved the
idea of getting out of Teaneck every day, I loved the idea of
being able to pay Ike, and Orli loved our new Chrysler
LeBaron convertible in forest green. Ike delicately suggested
we think about moving.

—You've got to get out of there, he said. —You need to
get away from your past.

—I need a full-time job.

Ike sighed. —I'm not telling you anything you don't
know.

—Then how do you explain these rates? I asked.

Three phone messages were waiting for me when I got
home: my sister-in-law had phoned, inviting us for Sabbath
dinner that evening; David Whateverstein had left a message inviting us over to their apartment for Sabbath lunch,
unaware that so had the Goldsomethings, who'd already
invited over the Whoeverblatts; and my mother had phoned,
wishing me a *gutten Shabbos,* which she knew I didn't
observe, and asking me to wish my brother the same when I
saw him at synagogue, which she knew I didn't attend.

I switched on the TV, turned down the volume, draped
the towel over the screen, and closed the window blinds.

—*Game seven, God,* I thought, —*don't screw around.*

We raced through dinner at my brother's house, and
made it home just in time for the start of the second period.
Seven seconds before the final buzzer, New Jersey scored and
sent the game into overtime. I leaned forward and glared at

heaven. At 4:24 of the second overtime, New York's left-winger Stephane Matteau rattled the puck in off the stick of the Devil's goalie.

—The Rangers, said Marv Albert, —are going to the Stanley Cup finals.

Orli and I screamed into our couch pillows, rolled on the floor, and shouted into balled-up bath towels. I cheered for the Rangers' aggressive offense. I cheered for their shrewd postseason trades. Most of all, I cheered for a God who maybe, just maybe, wasn't the prick they told me He was.

The deal I made with Him for the finals, against the Vancouver Canucks, was this: regardless of the outcome of games one and two, I would not watch game three (a Saturday). I wasn't offering that much up—in a seven-game series, it could never be a decisive game—but I'd begun to think that God had gotten a touch of Ranger fever Himself.

And by game four (a Tuesday), the Rangers were up 2–1. After seeing Ike that afternoon, I had some time before the next bus to Teaneck, and decided to walk to Port Authority. I passed Madison Square Garden, where I noticed a large crowd gathered on the arena's front steps.

—What's going on? I asked a nearby hot-dog vendor.

—Big game tonight, he said. —Hockey.

—Game's in Canada, I said, peering at the crowd across the street.

An excited man in a Rangers jersey pushed in beside me; in his hand was a placard that read "DESTINY."

—One with everything, he said to the vendor.

—Game's in Canada, I said to the Ranger fan.

—Away game, he said. —For five bucks, you can watch it on the Jumbotron.

The Garden was home ice for the Rangers, and tickets to a playoff game, if you could get them, cost a fortune. I'd heard of a man who'd paid $2,000 for a pair of seats behind the Rangers' net. —Fifty-four years! he had shouted, waving his tickets at the television news camera. —Fifty-four years!

—Go, Rangers! the man called, rushing off to the Garden.

—Go, Rangers! I called back.

I was too late to get tickets to that night's game, but game six (a Saturday) was also an away game. Friday morning I went to Madison Square Garden, where I paid ten dollars for two tickets. Why should God care whether I watched it on the seventeen-inch screen in my living room or on the Jumbotron hanging over center ice at the Garden? I simply had to make sure that I committed no more sins getting to the game than I would have at home.

—Rangers! Orli cheered when I showed her the tickets.

Teaneck felt like defeat. These tickets felt like rebellion, like life, and Orli cheered again.

I tried to calm her down.

—Listen, I said, —we're going to have to walk there.

Even with the money from my freelance work coming

in, funds were tight, and we could never afford a night in a Manhattan hotel. I thought for a moment we might be able to stay with friends, then remembered that we didn't have any; the only people I knew in Manhattan were the co-workers from my old job, whom Nick had once asked me to address in order to explain my absence from after-work gatherings on Friday nights.

—I'm married, I told them. —And we kind of observe Sabbath.

They didn't know what to say.

—You can't go to bars on Sabbath?

—No.

—Can you go to a concert?

—No.

—What can you do?

—Nothing.

—Why do you observe it?

I didn't know what to say.

—Rangers! Orli cheered again, jumping up and down in place.

—It's fourteen miles.

—RANGERS!

The next day, in order to avoid raising suspicion among our neighbors, Orli and I set out for New York in our Sabbath finest—me in my dress pants and a white button-down shirt, Orli in a blue dress and fancy shoes. In the bag I tried to conceal beneath my arm, I had our tickets, two Ranger hats, two Ranger jerseys (mine home, hers away), and some food for along the way.

And the children of Israel went up, harnessed, out of the land of Egypt.

It was a sweltering June morning. I was sweating heavily before we even reached the Teaneck town line. Mosquitoes sent by God surrounded my head; gnats dispatched a short while later attempted infiltration through my nose, as He had commanded them. We walked, single file, along Route 4, a six-lane interstate connecting New Jersey to New York City. Cars, trucks, and buses brushed past us at seventy miles an hour.

After an hour, we reached the George Washington Bridge. Here Route 4 merged with Route 80, and six lanes of traffic became eight, then ten, then twelve, a concrete maze of on-ramps, off-ramps, and cloverleafs. We climbed over a guardrail, bolted across two trucks-only lanes, climbed another guardrail, crossed a bus lane, and made for a small concrete island, where we waited for a break in traffic to allow us to cross the last three lanes to safety.

—They better win, I called out to Orli.

—What?

—I SAID THEY BETTER WIN.

Two tractor-trailers passed by, then a van and a couple of cars.

—Run! I shouted, and we took off.

By the time we crossed the George Washington Bridge

and followed the ramp to the West Side Highway, it was past three o'clock, and the sun was still getting stronger. You could have fried an egg on my head. (Cooking, category 11: Some rabbis say that if my head had been hot before Sabbath began, and the egg had been previously fried, you would be permitted to put the egg on my head in order to heat it up. Others disagree.)

We had planned to follow the highway straight down to Thirty-fourth Street, but the shoulder was far too treacherous. We climbed back up the ramp, crossed Riverside Drive, walked down 168th Street, turned right on Broadway, and headed downtown. Washington Heights became Spanish Harlem, Spanish Harlem became regular Harlem, and regular Harlem became the Upper West Side. We passed the San Juan Car Service, Puerto Rico Car Service, and Transportes Satolino. Los Muchachos Grocery and the Lechonera La Isla restaurant gave way to Ben's Kosher Deli, Benny's Kosher Pizza, and Benjy's Kosher Falafel, and we fought the desire to hail every cab that drove by. Old blisters popped. New blisters formed. God peered down, waiting, waiting.

—They better fucking win, I grumbled.

—They better fucking win, Orli agreed.

Exhaustion hit us hard at Fifty-ninth Street. We barely spoke. Each block felt like a mile. But as we reached Forty-second Street, we saw large groups of screaming hockey fans streaming down Broadway in their Ranger colors, clapping their hands and blowing their air horns. Taxicabs honked in time to the "Let's Go, Rangers" song. We pulled on our caps and jerseys and ran. We didn't stop until we were inside the Garden and settled into our seats, halfway up the arena, just to the left of center ice. Almost immediately, the Jumbotron lit up. Three thousand miles away, the Rangers took the ice, and we stood and cheered with all our might. Being in this enormous arena, surrounded by thousands of people shouting praise for people who weren't there, was the closest I'd felt to belonging in a very long time; it felt like synagogue—another place where people cheered for someone who wasn't there—but with hockey.

—*Fifty-four years,* I thought to God as I clapped and cheered and held my fists in the air. —*Do not screw around.*

It wasn't even close. The Vancouver goalie was nearly perfect, allowing only one Ranger goal the entire game. The Canucks had scored four.

—There's always game seven, said Orli.

But that wasn't the point, was it? I hadn't watched game three. I hadn't gotten in a cab or jumped on a bus. The point was that WE HAD A DEAL. The point was that I was living in a *shtetl* in New Jersey. I was giving it a shot, I was giving the whole damn thing another shot, and how many shots was He giving me? —*Tell me, God,* I thought as I sat there in Madison Square Garden, —*what line did I cross, what nonsensical, inscrutable law did I break that warranted this?* So I had carried a backpack (carrying, category 39). Was He serious? No way He was busting me on fucking *carrying.* I had walked a long way, that was true—one is forbidden to walk more than half a mile out of town on Sabbath—but, Jesus Christ, I wasn't the one who put Madison Square Garden on Thirty-fourth Street, was I?

—I'm not watching game seven, I said.

Orli sighed. —Don't be ridiculous, she said.

I stared at the floor, unable to bring myself to face her, and wondered how much longer she would be speaking to me at all. Was this why God had let her survive that first Ranger game of ours so many months ago? So I could drive her away myself? If the Rangers had won tonight, at least my insanity would have been validated. Now, as the Garden emptied, I had nothing.

We rode down the escalators in silence. What had I been thinking, playing the odds with this Guy? In God's casino, the house always wins—ask Moses, ask Job, ask Sarah—and there I was, sitting at the Lord's poker table, trying to count cards.

—What now? Orli asked once we'd made it outside.

All around us, people in non-Sabbath clothing jumped up and down on their non-blistered feet, shouting excitedly about the game—*What a series!*—and making predictions for game seven.

Across the street, on the far corner of Thirty-third, I spotted the hot-dog vendor I had spoken with the day before. I grabbed Orli by the hand and ran.

—Where are we going? she shouted.

We ran across the sidewalk, dodging hockey fans, and weaved our way through the taxicabs idling on Broadway.

—One with everything, I said to the vendor. —Extra *traif.*

Orli gasped.

The vendor handed me the hot dog, and I shoveled it straight into my mouth, forcing as much of it in as I could.

Orli screamed with glee.

—He hungry guy, the vendor said to Orli.

My cheeks stretched. My jaw ached. Mustard ran down my chin. I looked up at the sky, smiled at God as best I could, and gave Him the finger.

—Tashtes pfiggy, I managed to say.

I held the rest of the hot dog out to Orli, who raised her arms overhead in victory, dived forward, and took a vicious chomp off the end.

—Mmm, she said. —Non-kosher . . .

We laughed and hugged and tried to swallow without choking.

—Buck fifty, said the vendor.

I reached into my pocket and handed him a five. Orli pointed at the money and screamed.

—You carried money? she said. —*That's* why they lost!

In addition to the thirty-nine categories of work that are prohibited on Sabbath, the Sages also prohibited the touching or moving of anything—like money—that might lead to the thirty-nine categories of work.

—It was for an emergency! I pleaded, and we made our way toward Sixth Avenue to find a cab heading uptown.

I took another bite of my hot dog, grimaced, and threw it in the trash.

—Not as good as I thought it would be, I said.

—Wasting food? said Orli. —There goes game seven.

Her naïveté simply astounded me.

—He'll make them win, I said. —Just to stick it to me.

Three days later, on Tuesday, June 14, the Rangers won game seven of the 1994 Stanley Cup Championship by a final score of 3–2. I didn't watch the game. OK, fine, I watched the last period.

—Figures, I thought as Messier held the Stanley Cup over his head and circled the ice. —So predictable.

The following Saturday, Orli and I drove on the Sabbath for the very first time. We waited until after lunch, and when the Terrace Circle lawn finally cleared, we tiptoed downstairs, crept into our shiny new forest-green Chrysler LeBaron, and quietly drove out of the Terrace Circle parking lot. We hit Queen Anne Road, floored it, and drove to the Riverside Square Mall in Paramus, where we browsed awhile, talked about God, but couldn't bring ourselves to use money to make any purchases. The Sabbath after that we crept out again, this time to the Bergen Mall, where we browsed awhile, talked about God, bought some books and CDs, but left the packages in the car so that no one would see us carrying them in.

The advertising agency for which I had been freelancing had promised me a full-time job, and soon they delivered. Orli and I found an apartment on West Fifty-sixth Street, a one-bedroom non-Tudor, overlooking nothing, with no lawn out front. It was perfect.

The Sabbath after that, we walked to the Terrace Circle parking lot, climbed into the LeBaron, put the top down, and cranked up the music. We drove to Staples, where we bought some packing supplies, and then to Sixth Avenue Electronics, where we bought a nineteen-inch color TV for the new apartment. It was just after one o'clock in the afternoon when we returned, and everyone was out on the lawn, walking off the Sabbath meal. We strode in slow motion across the grass—Orli with her arms full of Staples shopping bags, me struggling with a nineteen-inch color TV—past the couples with babies and the couples without babies holding the babies of the couples with babies, and they all stared and gasped and shook their heads. Mrs. Whateverberg sat scowling on the bench beside the door to our building. I winked as we walked by.

—Nineteen inches, I whispered, —cable ready. *Im yirtzeh Hashem* by you.

Welcome to Virtual Jerusalem!

SEND A PRAYER

As the new Jewish New Year approaches, we are urged to open our hearts in prayer. In light of the pain and loss of the people of Israel, this year it seems our prayers may be more powerful than ever before. Pray for the souls of the victims of terror, and for their families whose lives are forever altered.

WHAT IS THE WESTERN WALL?

The Western Wall, or Kotel, is the only surviving remnant of the Temple that stood in Jerusalem. The Temple served as the closest connecting spot between the Jewish people and God. During the exile that followed the destruction of the Temple, prayer remained as the only means available to maintain a divine connection.

NOTES IN THE WALL

A tradition developed of writing a few lines of prayer on a note to be placed inside the cracks of the soft old stones of the Western Wall. Many send notes, or kvitelach, *when they hear of someone making a trip to the Kotel.*

MODERN TECHNOLOGY ALLOWS VIRTUAL JERUSALEM TO FACILITATE THE PROCESS!

Whatever your message, we will place your prayer among the countless others: a testament to the connection between God, Israel, and the Jewish people that refuses to be extinguished. Your prayers will be collected every week and taken down to the Wall by VirtualJerusalem.com staffers.

To send a note to the Western Wall, please log in, fill in the form below, and send:

Your name

Your e-mail

Your prayer (limit 200 chars)

Six weeks before our scheduled due date, we still hadn't come to a decision about whether to circumcise our son. We hadn't been discussing it much—ixnay on the oreskinfay—but I had gone online and quietly continued my research. I discovered that during the ceremony an empty chair, reserved for the angel Elijah, is placed near the child, for it is said that so important to God is the ancient ritual that when a man circumcises his son, God calls upon the angels and proudly says, —Come and see what my sons are doing in the world, and Elijah descends to the Earth to witness the moment on God's behalf (Zohar, 1:93). I discovered that even Frasier Crane circumcised his son (season 8, episode 167), and he was married to a non-Jew. And I discovered the SmartKlamp, a clear plastic at-home circumcision device that looks like a corkscrew designed by Philippe Starck. It avoids, according to its website, the problems often associated with circumcision, such as "infection of the circumcised wound . . . postoperative bleeding . . . cutting the glans of the penis . . . part amputation of the penis . . ." and risk of removal of too much, or not enough, of the foreskin.

Come and see what your sons are doing in the world.

We went for a hike.

—Do you want to do this? I asked Orli.

—I don't know. Do you?

—I don't know.

—So the chair's for Elijah? she asked.

—Apparently.

—I didn't know that.

—Me neither.

—God can't watch it for Himself?

—I don't think that's the point.

—I thought He could see everything.

—He can.

—So what's Elijah for?

—Nothing. Pictures. Cake. How the fuck should I know? He brings back a nice piece of cake.

—Is that also in the Zohar? That God loves cake?

—Yes, it is. Twinkies.

—Is that why He made them non-kosher?

—Probably. He's very selfish.

—Do you want to do this?

—I don't know. You?

—I don't know.

And I also discovered VirtualJerusalem.com, where I composed a virtual prayer note for someone to cram into a non-virtual wall to a virtual God who might kill my non-virtual son because I'd eaten bacon with virtually every egg since I was nineteen, or because I drove on Sabbath, or because I wrote things about God that He didn't approve of. It was worth a shot.

> *Dear God,*
>
> *Please don't kill my son during birth. Also, don't kill my wife during birth. And don't kill him after birth. And please make him healthy, and don't fuck around and make him seem sick just to scare me. I know you're probably pissed at me, but I'm pissed at You, too, so let's just keep this between us. Thanks. S.*

That was 262 characters, not including spaces. I dropped the bit about God fucking around to try and scare me, and that got me down to 212. I missed the part about letting God know I was wise to His little scare tactics, but at last this version was down to 184 characters without spaces, 225 with. Was the 200-character limit including spaces? It didn't say, and I didn't want to risk it. That was just the kind of fast one God would pull—my son would die and I would kill myself and I'd go to heaven and say, —What the fuck? and He'd be like, —E-mail? I didn't get any e-mail. Must have been over the character limit. And all the asshole angels would laugh.

> *Dear God,*
> *Please don't kill my son during birth. And don't kill*
> *my wife during birth. I know You're probably pissed at*
> *me, but I'm pissed at You, too, so let's just keep this*
> *between us. Thanks. S.*

It lost a lot of the original, but I was down to 196 characters including spaces. At the last minute I chickened out, and took out the whole "pissed" section.

> *Dear God,*
> *Please don't kill my son. Or my wife. Thanks. S.*

Dread is the soul of brevity.

There was a problem.
—Shoulder, said the midwife, shaking her head. —Stuck.

—*Here we go,* I thought. —*Here we fucking fucking fucking go.*

His head was out, along with his right arm, reaching overhead, dipping his hand into the waters of the world, testing it before diving in.

—*Feels cold, Dad.*

—*It gets colder, kid.*

Orli and I had spent the last nine Tuesday nights in birth classes. The first three weeks we learned about every possible complication during labor, and about how each one could kill our baby. The second three weeks were spent learning about every possible medical treatment of the complications discussed during the first three weeks, and during the final three weeks we learned about how every one of the possible medical treatments mentioned in the middle three weeks could kill our baby. Then they gave us a photo album and a diaper.

I held Orli's hand. Our son's face was blue. Getting bluer.

—What do you see? she managed between breaths.

—Nothing, I said.

—*Moses,* I thought.

The tease. The peek. A glimpse. This is how this joke of His works. A blue head, a blue-black arm, Moses' pre-mortem peek of the Promised Land—*he's got Orli's lips*—an oldie but a goodie, O Lord—*he's so blue*—an oldie but a goodie. Orli asks, —What's going on? I didn't know. I didn't know how much time we had to get him out, I didn't know—*he's blue he's blue*—what the nurses were shouting to one another, I didn't know what the red light meant, the one—*he's so blue*—that had just lit up on the wall beside her bed, I didn't know what the steel table was for, the one that they had just had rolled in, the one with the clear plastic box on top—*do something*—and the gray tubes and the yellow cords tied around and clamped together as if the whole thing had just been pulled out of the back of some storage closet most nurses had never even seen because the level of badness of a situation rarely—*do something*—reached the level where you might need a machine such as this, whatever this machine was, and I didn't know why—*for God's sake, do something*—a nurse was climbing onto the delivery bed, and I didn't know why she was pressing on Orli's pelvis with her knee, and then Orli was moaning and the midwife was shaking her head and the nurse was shaking her head and she put her second knee on Orli's pelvis and I didn't know what she was doing but, Jesus Christ, she was all out of fucking knees, if knees are some kind of answer, we're going to need more knees because mine are shaking too hard to be of any use.

—Got him, called the midwife. —Got him, got him, got him, keep pressing, keep pressing, got him, got him.

I wiped the sweat from Orli's brow and I laughed, and I closed my eyes and rested my head against Orli's, and I thought about that expression, the one about God giving unto whoever a son, and about how little it felt like that, how much it felt as if we'd stolen a son from Him, ripped it from His hands—that was what that laugh was, the same laugh I had when I walked out of Macy's with a bag full of clothes—how at best He dangled it over our heads for a while and made us jump for it like a child for candy as He laughed at our ache and struggle. But give? It didn't feel as if He'd *given* us anything. It felt as if He'd lost His grip. Like He'd given up. Like He'd let the babies have their baby.

—He's not breathing, said the midwife.

—*I'm sorry,* I said to God. —*I'm sorry, I'm sorry, holy fucking shit, I'm fucking sorry.*

Which isn't why we circumcised him. Or maybe it was. I don't know.

—It happens, said the midwife later.

His airways had been blocked. She had suctioned his nose and mouth, ventilated him, and he soon began breathing on his own.

The following day the doctor came in and, after some routine checks on our baby, he asked us if we intended to circumcise him.

—We guess, said Orli.

Thanks for nothing, Google. For every medical reason not to circumcise, there seemed to be a reason to circumcise him. For every psychological reason to circumcise him, there seemed to be a psychological reason not to.

We had the doctor do it. At least there was no God involved.

—Follow me, said the doctor.

Following, leaving, journeying. It still wasn't over.

And Abraham arose . . . and he went forth. According to many, this was Abraham's defining moment: the moment he looked around, saw what the world around him had become, and behold, he did leave, saying, —Fuck this. For this he is considered by the followers of the world's major religions to be their father, followers who laud his courage and strength of spirit in one breath, and threaten, in the next, any of their flock who might be foolish enough to consider going forth themselves. As I pushed my son's bassinet down the hall, I wondered if this leaving, this searching for something new, this disillusionment with the choices available, is, for some of us, the essential fucked-up condition of our lives. I wondered if we are all foreskins now. And if Abraham were alive today—in Monsey, or Mecca, or Vatican City—I wondered if he wouldn't arise in the morning, pack up his camel, and say, —Fuck this, all over again.

—It's okay, said the doctor as he rolled our son into the exam room. —I did all my own sons.

—We do our own taxes, I said.

—You're very funny, laughed the doctor.

I pictured him tied to a stake; I pictured pulling up the skin on top of his shiny, bald head and snipping it off. I pictured rolling his skin all the way down his body as he screamed and screamed and begged for mercy, and, once it lay there piled up at his bloody feet, I made Kiddush on a goblet of wine and had a piece of cake.

—Very, very funny, he said.

I pressed my hands to my ears and turned around. My son screamed. I closed my eyes. Synagogues burned. Torahs were torn to shreds. Gods were banished. The moment my son became a Jew was the moment I felt, more than I had ever before in my life, that I was not.

I went home the following afternoon to feed the dogs, get some decent food for Orli, and check my e-mail. In the days since the birth, I began to wonder if maybe God had saved our son. If maybe he was supposed to be born stillborn, but God intervened. If He had answered my prayers. If the note had worked. I logged on to Virtual Jerusalem, and found the Send a Prayer page. This was going to be more of a thank-you than a prayer, but they didn't have a separate page for that. I filled in my name, typed out my e-mail address, and in the message box below, wrote, simply:

> *Thank you.*
> *S.*

I was about to hit the send button when a flashing yellow text box at the bottom of the page caught my attention.

Due to a system failure, read the note, *all notes sent to the Wailing Wall during the past several weeks have been lost. The system is now functioning normally and we apologize for the technical error.*

The phone rang. It was my mother. I thought I was delivering good news.

—What's his name? my mother asked.

—Paix, I said.

—Max?

—Paix.

—What kind of name is Paix?

—Thanks, I said. —We like it, too.

—Max, with an *m*?

—Paix. With a *p*. And an *i*. It means "peace." Like my name, but without the God bit.

—Why would you name your kid "peace"?

—What?

—Who names their kid "peace"?

—You named your kid "peace."

—I named my kid "peace"? Who did I name "peace"?

—Me. You named me "peace."

Soon after my brother Jeffie died, my sister was diagnosed with deafness in one ear. I was born two years later, and so, my mother had explained when I was younger, she had named me Shalom; I was to be their peace.

—I didn't name you "peace," she said.

—My name means "peace," Mom.

—Yeah, but that's not why we named you it.

Pause.

—Does he have a Hebrew name?

—No.

—Oh.

Pause.

—May I ask if there'll be a *bris*?

I thought I was delivering good news.

—Yeah, yeah. We had the doctor do it.

—The doctor?

—In the hospital.

—When?

—Yesterday.

—Yesterday?

—Yes.

—When was he born?

—Two days ago.

—Oh.

And that's when the meconium really hit the fan.

According to someone, the circumcision needs to happen on the eighth day, and it needs to be performed by a God-fearing, Torah-observant Jew; and the God-fearing, Torah-observant Jew needs to place his lips upon the wound and suck blood from it, and I need to say, —"Blessed are You, Lord our God, King of the universe, who has sanctified us with His commandments and commanded us to enter him into the Covenant of Abraham our father."

I felt as if I had gotten the right answer on the final round of *Jeopardy!* but had forgotten to phrase the answer as a question.

It was the foreskin that broke the camel's back.

21.

Shalom—
I was thinking of coming up to see the baby on Sunday.
I can be there by two, and I would love to see him.
—Mom

Samuel Beckett was often accused of being a pessimist, a charge he denied. In fact, he argued, those who are labeled pessimists are the true optimists—were it not for their belief that the world, however awful, could be improved, they would never bother raising the issues. Optimists, he further argued, are the true pessimists in that they're so convinced the situation is beyond repair, all they can do is pretend there's nothing wrong with it.

—I think this will go well, I called out to Orli. She was downstairs with Paix.

No answer.

—Seriously, I said. —I'm not just being optimistic.

Nothing. I listened carefully. No baby sounds. Were they dead? Did God kill them? Did he make her kill the baby and then kill herself? Was it because of this visit? Was I standing here, calling out how well I thought the visit would go, when their dead bodies were downstairs turning blue and getting . . .

—Did you say something? Orli asked as she walked into the bedroom.

—You okay?

—Yeah. Why?

—Nothing. I hate this fucking house. You can't hear a thing.

—Some people pay extra for that, said Orli. —What did you say?

—I said I thought this visit would go well.

She laughed.

Fifteen minutes later, I watched from the window as my father struggled with a large, brightly colored gift-wrapped box that he had taken from the back of his station wagon. I hadn't seen them in quite a while. They both looked old. Time was running out. For what, I didn't know.

I could see my father's teeth clenching, his same old face turning the same old red. He pulled open the front door and, cursing under his breath, shoved the box through the doorway and onto the floor. He kicked it into the foyer, raised a hand to one of my dogs, wisely thought better of it (they hunt lions), ignored Orli's attempt at a hug hello, and walked into the dining room, where he stood in the corner, arms folded across his chest as he stared through dark sunglasses out the dining room window. Neither he nor my mother took off their coats.

Good times.

My mother would not say Paix's name. She asked how "the baby" was, said how cute "the baby" looked, and asked how well "the baby" was doing. If we'd named him Yankel Berel Shmerel, she would have had it sewn on her T-shirt in sequins.

—He's cute, isn't he? she said to my father.

Nothing.

—Oh, he is! she continued. —Did you ever see such a head of hair!

Nothing.

She reminded me of a woman in a war zone, sweeping the kitchen floor and dusting the china as bombs exploded around her. —*I must get this place cleaned up, the dinner guests will be here any minute!*

—Who do you think he looks like? she asked my father.

—He looks like a baby, my father grumbled.

They left. I watched them go. I had the distinct feeling that I was standing on a pier that had suddenly been cut loose from its moorings and I was slowly drifting out to sea.

It was a pleasant feeling.

It would be the last time I saw them.

My sister e-mailed me a week later to tell me I was the smallest piece of sh&t in the world, and while nobody in the family gives a f$ck what I do, would it have been so d&mn hard to circumcise my son on the eighth day?

Substituting symbols for vowels in forbidden words is a common loophole of the devout. When they're not preaching what a Fucking Maniac the Lord is, they're behaving like He's a Fucking Idiot.

—Fuck you, I responded. —And the Tor@h you rode in on.

My mother e-mailed me next. I had broken the covenant with Abraham, she declared. She listed the things I had done to hurt her: violating Sabbath, getting tattoos, the things I'd written, the things I had published or planned to. By the end of the note, she was going Holocaust: by keeping my son from his family and his roots, I was denying my son safe harbor in Israel when the next Holocaust arrived. She ended with a hopeful quotation from the prophet Jeremiah, wherein he promises that one day the sinners shall be punished and that those who have gone astray will repent and be returned to their mothers.

I thought that was ironic. Jeremiah never married. He never had to circumcise his own son. According to legend, neither did his parents, as Jeremiah had been born circumcised. So why don't you shut the fuck up, Jerry?

Thousands of years ago, a terrified, half-mad old man genitally mutilated his son, hoping it would buy him some points with the Being he hoped was running the show. Over the years, equally terrified men wrote blessings and composed prayers and devised rituals and ordained that an empty seat be left for Elijah. Six thousand years later, a father will not look his grandson in the face, and a mother and sister will defend such behavior, because the child wasn't mutilated in precisely the right fashion.

Come see what your sons are doing in the world.

I phoned Ike. I asked him for an appointment. I took a train into the city.

—Why don't you try writing back to her? he suggested.

Three hundred fifty dollars an hour.

Oy vey, the letter began. She mentioned Abraham, I mentioned Isaac, the son who never recovered—the pensive forefather a nation of faithful conveniently forget grew into a man who rarely spoke, whose trauma left him passive, easily victimized, a man of inaction who seemed never to rebound from the admirable non-self-sacrifice of his esteemed father— and here I was, being sacrificed on the same altar, to the same God, except this time there was no ram in the thickets.

Have a gutten shmutten butten whatever, I wrote. *I'll be in the woods with my family.*

I didn't send the letter.

I didn't print it.

I rolled a joint.

I didn't smoke it.

Come see, You Fuck. Come see what Your sons are doing in the world.

I went downstairs to see if my son was dead.

He wasn't.

22.

*I*t is a few days from my son's first birthday, and I am sitting in a local Woodstock café, waiting to speak with the owner about a cake I would like him to bake for the party we are planning. A young man enters, sits down at a table near the window, and begins reading his newspaper. When the waiter approaches, the man asks if the waiter wouldn't mind turning the music off.

—I need . . . I need to think, he says. —You know, and in order to think I need to connect, you know, spiritually, internally, I need to find my way to my inner source and it's very disturbing, because thought is a bubble, your spirit and inner space, you know?

—Sure, says the waiter.

After a moment, the man spots a woman at a table nearby. She has long Pippi Longstocking braids and wears a floral dress and Birkenstock sandals.

I have just described everyone in Woodstock.

—What are you drawing? he asks.

—Something from a dream, she says in a spiritual whisper. —I had a dream and I saw the Christ, and he was resurrected, only his body wasn't filled with skin and bones and pain and agony. It was filled with rainbows.

—Rainbows?

—Mmm-hmm. And the rainbows were love. And they filled the world.

—That's beautiful, he said.

He moved to her table, handed her his business card, and pressed her to come to his film, which he was screening that night at a local pub. She handed him her business card, in case he wanted his skull read and his chakra mapped. Or his chakra read and his skull mapped. I forget.

Woodstock is a thriving tourist town known around the world for something that didn't actually happen there; the famous music festival took place in Bethel, a non-thriving town not famous anywhere for something that actually did happen there.

Pictures do not represent actual contents.

Orli and I moved here ten years ago. We live just outside of Woodstock, on a mountain that overlooks a valley. We have loved it here. We have walked hundreds of miles through the forests, first just the two of us, then with Harley, then with Harley and Duke, now with the dogs running ahead and our son strapped to my back. I hate parades, but I love this one. In recent years, the town has changed, or we have changed, or both. It has become the art version of

Vegas. Artists name themselves Love and Peace and Free, and sell oversized, overpriced canvases featuring brightly colored flowers and brightly colored doves and brightly colored people holding hands, canvases that barely fit in the overpriced, oversized Hummers of their Manhattan customers. People wear tie-dyed shirts with Diesel jeans, BMW sports cars wear stickers reminding the Lexus sports cars behind them about the tragedy in Darfur. In the back of our minds, we know the search for our Promised Land is not yet over, and may never be.

The owner of the café arrives, and we talk cake.

—What kind of cake do you want? he whines.

Homosexuality is revered in this town, less so for the homosexual's defiant refusal to be told whom he or she may love, more so for his or her taste in wine and home furnishings. Because of this, many men here affect a certain degree of stereotypical homosexuality, which in turn causes the homosexual men here to affect an even greater degree of such. Down the road at the Kingston Mall, white kids are pretending they're black, and black kids are pretending to be West Coast gangsters. We are all lost, each in our own terrifying, ludicrous desert that seems to stretch on for eternity.

—I don't care, I said. —One big enough to fit this on it.

I hand him a sheet of paper.

—You want all this on a cake? he asks.

I nod.

He reads the paper and gives me a sidelong glance.

—Cheer *up*, he whines.

. . .

It rained the afternoon of Paix's birthday, but nothing could dampen my spirits. I'd traveled into Manhattan to see Ike, and decided to check in first at the agency.

—So, said Craig, —a year, huh?

—Unbelievable, I said, settling into his couch.

—And Paix?

—Great.

—And the writing?

—Going well. Haven't deleted anything in weeks.

—I'm happy for you, said Craig.

—Thanks. I'm fucked, of course.

—Of course, said Craig. —God must be cooking up something really big.

—I'm guessing something with an explosion.

—Something disfiguring.

—Probably.

—But not deadly.

—No.

—He wouldn't let you off that easy.

—No, no. He'll burn my face off and then curse me with a long life.

—Well, said Craig, —if it means anything to you, I hope He kills you quickly.

—You're a good friend, I said.

My session with Ike felt like a victorious team meeting in the locker room after a long, difficult game. How different

I was from the time when, ten years earlier, I had first stepped into his office. In that time, I had distanced myself from a destructive family while managing somehow to build a loving one around myself at the same time. Orli and I had once feared that our child would drag the past back into the present, and it was clear now, on the afternoon of his first birthday, that he had been the very thing we'd needed to head into the future once and for all.

Ike smiled and told me how proud he was of the progress I had made in our time together. I invited him to join us for the birthday party, though I knew he could never make it to Woodstock in time.

—Thank you, though, said Ike. —I wish I could. Save me a piece of cake.

I showed him the message I had the baker put on the cake. Ike raised his eyebrows and squinted.

—Is that going to fit on a Cookiepuss? he asked.

When I got home, Paix was in the driveway, stomping in rain puddles and squatting down beside overturned newts.

—Newt, he said. —Uh-oh.

I went inside and tried to get a little writing done before the guests arrived.

—Dada! he called.

I ignored him.

—Dada! he called again.

—What?

—Dada!

—WHAAAAT?

—DADA! he called.

He'd made his way into the bedroom and was standing beside my chair, his head cocked to get my attention. This is a game we play—he calls my name and I lean over in his face and pretend to shout "WHAAAAT?" as loudly as I can. Then he runs away and I chase him. He'll claim credit for it, but I totally made it up.

—Dada! he said.

—What?

—Dada!

—WHAAAAT?

He laughed—Ahhhh!—and ran off, and I closed my laptop, slid it under the bed, and took off after him, his head of crazy curls disappearing into the kitchen.

—I'm . . . gonna . . . GET YOU!

God's dirtiest trick yet.

Orli went into the kitchen and called everyone to the table. I held Paix in my arms. It reminded me of the sacrifice of Isaac, the sharp knife so near a child. I wondered if Abraham and Sarah ever had birthday parties for Isaac. I imagined them a lot like the birthdays of my youth—Sarah lighting a candle and baking some bread, Abraham somewhere behind the tent, fixing jugs or working on the camels.

—Cocksucker, Abraham muttered.

Orli brought out the cake, placed it on the table, and went to get some plates.

—Jesus Christ, said my friend Jack.

Happy birthday, Paix, read the cake. *From Mommy, Daddy, Harley, Duke, and no one else in our families because they are bitter miseries who'd rather drag us into the morass of their bleak, tragic lives than share for a moment in our joy. And many more.*

—Who wants the "bleak"? asked Orli.

—Give me a slice of "tragic," said Jack.

I've been thinking about the people in my life now, and here's what I think: I think they're all foreskins. Jack's a foreskin; his mother brutalized him, cast him off, cut him repeatedly. Alisha is a foreskin, and her husband, Will, is, too. So am I. So is Orli. A little foreskin nation, trying their best to start over, build up, move on.

Soon it was time for Paix to go to bed, and I stared at him in his crib and thought of Moses, and of the bassinet in which he was discovered, floating among the reeds by the side of the Nile, and of the lifelong journey he made to a Promised Land, a land of God, a land he never quite reached. My Promised Land, the one I had been stumbling around looking for these past thirty years, would be one with no God, at least not with the God I knew, and I realized then that, like Moses, I would probably never get there, either. But my son—he might just have a shot.

And the people did rejoice to see the Promised Land to which they had come, and they did sing and dance and cheer, and Moses, facedown in the sand and clutching his chest, did look up, and smiled to see his children so happy and so free. And the Lord said unto Moses, —This is the land I promised. I have let you see it with your eyes but you will not cross over into it. And Moses did say, —Blow me, and he died there in the desert with a smile upon his face.

I kissed Paix good night and went back upstairs. We sat upstairs in the living room, just me, Orli, a few bottles of wine, and some of our closest foreskins, talking about our families, broken, bitter, and belligerent all. It was past midnight by the time the last of them stumbled from the house, and we shut off the lights and went to bed. I lay in the dark, listening to Orli breathing and thinking—about my son, about my wife, about the suggestion someone earlier had made that perhaps the Promised Land wasn't a physical space at all, but mostly about how silent the baby monitor had been for the past few minutes. Too silent.

I threw off my covers, hurried downstairs, and opened my son's bedroom door as quietly as I could. Paix lifted his head and smiled.

—Dada, said Paix.

—Hey, buddy, I whispered. —Shh. Go to sleep.

I closed the door and sighed, and then raced upstairs, two steps at a time, figuring the whole dead-kid thing had been a trap and it was Orli who was dead.

I believe in God.

It's been a real problem for me.

Orli stirred when I entered the room, and I climbed quietly back into bed.

—Not dead, is he? she mumbled.

—No, I whispered. —Neither are you.

—Good. I have Ike tomorrow.

She buried her face in her pillow, and took my hand in hers.

—They really did a number on you, she said.

I gave her hand a squeeze, turned up the volume on the baby monitor, and tried to sleep.

Whom to Kill

The one thing I've found that most religious people agree upon—Jews, Christians, and Muslims alike—is that if you meet them, and you're having a little conversation and you say, for instance, —God's a prick, they tend to react badly.

Which I find surprising.

Because they're the ones who told me He was. They told me all about Him—about the floods, the pillars of salt, the killing, the slaughtering, that He was quick to anger yet full of mercy, that He was stiff-necked but forgiving, that He flew off the eternal handle with frightening regularity—that He was, basically, a prick. And I believed them. I still do. So, God, I beg you, please don't kill my wife because of this book. Don't kill my son, and don't kill my dogs. If you absolutely must kill somebody, kill Geoff Kloske at Riverhead Books. Kill Ira Glass at *This American Life,* and while you're there, kill Julie Snyder and Sarah Koenig, too. Kill David Remnick at *The New Yorker,* and kill Carin Besser, who's just down the hall. Kill Sara Ivry at Nextbook.org, and you might as well kill Jessa Crispin at Bookslut.com. Kill Craig Markus for helping with the cover art, and kill Ike Herschkopf if you really have to, but don't kill me. And don't kill Orli. And don't kill our son. It's just a fucking book.

Sorry.